COINS
AS LIVING
HISTORY

COINS AS LIVING HISTORY

Ted Schwarz

Ted Schwarz (signature)

ARCO PUBLISHING COMPANY, INC.
New York

Published by Arco Publishing Company, Inc.
219 Park Avenue South, New York, N.Y. 10003

Library of Congress Catalog Card Number 75-2708
ISBN 0-668-03791-1

100623

Printed in the United States of America

Contents

Introduction

If you take a few coins from your pocket, what do you have? Some circular pieces of metal stamped with different designs? A down payment on a meal at your favorite restaurant? Or perhaps the cost of the latest motion picture? No matter how you view your pocket change, I doubt if you hold it in very high regard.

There is more to your coins than you might imagine, however. The pocket change most of us have viewed so casually all our lives has far more meaning than just the value of the metal it contains. Coins have been a major force in helping to advance civilization. They permitted the division of labor that has allowed society to industrialize. In ancient times they spread news of major construction projects, changes in political leadership, and other important events. They have served as mininewspapers, objects of art, and even sources of propaganda. It might well be said that for over 2,000 years, coinage has been a miniature mirror of the story of mankind.

Barter was the means of exchange for ancient civilizations. If one family had wheat and another family had cows, they would get together and try to decide how much grain was a fair exchange for each cow. Trade was arbitrary and values were often decided at the time of bartering. Ten bushels of wheat might buy a cow one month, while eight bushels might buy a similar cow from the same family in a different month.

Such early trade kept men close to the land and close to their homes. If all you owned were chickens, you couldn't risk taking them to a different part of the country because you couldn't be sure that anyone would be interested in trading for them. You knew that near your home you could get the vegetables you did not grow from a neighbor who enjoyed an occasional chicken dinner. But if you took a few hens and went traveling, you would have a sparse diet if people in the territory you were visiting did not value your chickens enough to trade for them.

In order to allow a certain amount of freedom of movement it was decided that necessary goods should have consistent values. At first values were expressed in the form of tools and weapons of war. For example, everyone needed an axe no matter where he lived. If the axe was used as a standard, then a man could know that two of his chickens were worth two axes. He could take his chickens to the vegetable grower and ask for the number of vegetables that were the equivalent of two axes; this was a set amount which did not vary anywhere.

Later, tools and weapons were abandoned as the media of exchange. Cattle seemed more important, so goods and even services were rated in terms of cows. A week's physical toil might be worth half a cow, for example, or a crop of corn would be worth ten cows. Unfortunately this system failed to take into consideration whether the cow was big or small, strong or sickly, old or young. The concept was good but a standard was lacking. To make matters worse, it was difficult for some people to keep cattle. Wealth became as great a burden as poverty.

The concept of coinage evolved slowly. Once coins became common, people had a freedom they had never experienced before. A farmer could sell his crops and receive bits of metal in exchange. He could then place the metal pieces in his pocket and travel to a far off city where he could use the coins to rent a place to sleep and obtain a meal. He was no longer forced to stay at home to be certain his barter objects would be accepted by others. Coins gave him the freedom to travel unencumbered and without fear. He could obtain goods and services wherever he went, always at fixed rates. He could become an artist, a shoemaker, a wagon maker, or take up any other non-agricultural profession, secure in the knowledge that the coins he received for his work would enable him to eat as well as when he lived on a farm.

And so our story begins. Let us now examine the true stories told by and about coins that make them a living history.

1

In the Beginning

It might be said that had it not been for domestication of the horse, the world would never have developed a system of coinage. Before man first learned to ride, travel was extremely limited. Communities were self-sufficient, doing without the goods and services that could not be obtained within a few miles of their settlements.

In 1800 B.C., soldiers on horseback began to venture far from their homes to capture other civilizations. The Syrian Hyksos, for example, took control of Egypt, introducing the horse to people who had formerly relied on the slow moving camel and mule.

During the next 200 years the Egyptians regained their freedom and learned to adapt the horse to their own needs. By 1600 B.C., caravans of traders were taking goods into lands they had never before visited. They still relied on the slow moving donkeys and camels to haul their merchandise, but they no longer had to stay close to home for fear that robbers would take their goods. Their caravans were protected by armed men on horseback who could swiftly put any attackers to flight. Regular trade routes throughout the known world were finally established.

Barter had long been the accepted method for doing business, but the traders soon found that trade between nations was quite different from trade within one or two near-by communities. When they traded close to home, all the people valued goods in the same manner; but when they went to other countries matters were quite different. The Egyptians traded with gold, silver, bronze, and electrum, the latter being a mixture of silver and gold found in nature. The Hittites would accept some silver for trading but generally wanted to barter with cattle. The people of Cyprus had no common ground with the others since their trading had always been done with copper ingots. Obviously, some common standards had to be devised or trading would be impossible.

The initial standard for these nations was the ox. It was an animal everyone had and valued so they related all of their barter goods in terms of oxen. For example, 60 pounds of copper might be worth one animal, as would a small bar of gold.

To further indicate value, some countries cast bronze and copper representations of an oxhide, each figure equal in intrinsic value to one ox. These units were called *talanton* by the Greeks, with each individual piece known as a *talent*.

Gradually each country developed barter objects based on weight. The largest weight would be equal to the ox, for example. There were also smaller pieces of valued metals, each worth a fraction of the ox.

The talanton and similar ingots were not coins, but, since they represented wealth, a system of banking was soon developed to handle large transactions. Kings and merchants used special treasure houses in both palaces and sacred temples for the storage of ingots of gold and other precious metals. These were well guarded and accurate records were maintained, generally on clay tablets, telling of deposits and withdrawals.

At first only the elite had storehouses of this type. Later, however, the Semites decided that everyone should have access to such protection so they began accepting deposits of ingots from anyone who would pay a fee for the privilege. Soon loans were being made—for an additional fee—intended to cover the occasional person who was unable to repay the borrowed ingots.

And so the world saw the development of banks, loan companies, and similar services before anyone had invented coinage as we know it. That step was first taken by the Lydians, but it was the Greeks who raised it to an art form and then spread it throughout the known world.

Coinage as we know it began in the seventh century B.C. At first the pieces of precious metal were related to the barter object in much the same way as the earlier ingots. For example, we now say that a cow is worth so many dollars. The Greeks would have said that the dollar was worth so many cows. The barter object was the standard by which the coins were valued.

The earliest coins are generally stamped with the image of a barter object of equal value. The coins of Athens show a picture of an olive sprig and we know that the growing of olives was a major enterprise of that state.

Similar approaches were used in other areas. The sea turtle shell was the common barter object in Aegina, so their coins were marked with the design of the tortoise. Wine cups were used on coins of the Isle of Naxos, each coin equal to a measure of the liquid. The gold talent, changed to a coin, bore the image of a cow.

Once the public was accustomed to using coins in trade, the designs became more complex. Some of them adopted the emblems and seals of city governments. These designs were reminiscent of the seals of authority which were once used by leaders in Babylonia, Assyria, and Egypt. Merchants, rulers, and the elite among the citizens used signet rings and cylinder seals which were pressed or rolled in wax and clay to affix an authoritative mark on objects.

Other coins had drawings which were puns on the issuing city's name. The coins of Ankona showed the elbow, or "ankon," while the coins of Trapezos showed the table of "trapeza."

Later coins showed drawings of the gods, a tremendous artistic challenge for the designers. When they switched to portraits of humans, they tried to be as exact as they could in preparing the likenesses.

By the fifth century B.C., coins were produced showing elaborate drawings of people and animals in action. Many of these pieces reflect artistic achievement equal to the larger works of sculpture that have been so highly prized through the centuries.

In some cases the early Greek coins have provided us with information which would otherwise have been lost. The Colossus of Rhodes, one of the seven wonders of the ancient world, was a 100- to 115-foot statue of the sun god, Helios. It stood atop the harbor at Rhodes and was a familiar landmark to merchants. Unfortunately it was ruined during an earthquake in 224 B.C., but we know how it appeared through a copy which forms the obverse on a series of ancient coins.

When the Louvre Museum acquired the pieces of the statue Nike, the Winged Victory of Samothrace, the remains were reassembled by studying the statue as it was depicted on the obverse of a coin issued in 303 B.C. by Demetrius Poliorcetes of Macedon.

The first coins were made of gold, silver, and electrum. They were large in size and were meant only for paying soldiers and making sizeable purchases.

The concept of "small change" was developed by individual towns which produced miniature versions of the larger coins. The drachma was the standard, and the cities produced the obol and half-obol equal to 1/6 and 1/2 drachma, respectively. Later the onkia was added. This coin,

The Athenian owl, the first widely used coin.

equaling 1/10 obol, was struck in bronze, and its use was limited to Sicily for the first hundred years of its existence.

Coins did aid traders traveling from community to community, but at first there was no consistency in the degree of acceptance. Coins were considered profit-making items through taxation and other methods. For example, a state might issue a coin containing enough gold to buy a cow in most parts of the country. It could then arbitrarily change the value so a profit over and above the cost of production would be made. Coins had to be spent as marked in dealings with the government, but merchants were not so restricted. They would weigh the coins and sell their goods based on the intrinsic worth. This value was tied to the money standards for that particular state. In other words, a coin which could buy a cow in one area might be worth two cows somewhere else. It was quite a while before coins were given universally accepted values.

Coins were a blessing for the restless youths of Greece. No longer were they tied to the land where their families lived. They could stop being concerned about having barter objects that would be acceptable only to their neighbors. Instead of earning an ox or other animal for a week's work, they could receive coins which would have a value anywhere they went. True, the value might fluctuate but at least the coins could be spent wherever the young people might travel. They could go to other cities or, if they preferred, take their wages and use them for drink. If they still wanted animals, they were not restricted to the animals available in the immediate vicinity. They could buy any type they desired from wherever such creatures could be obtained.

Greece had just one source of precious metal—the silver mines at Laurium under the control of the government in Athens. As a result, the largest number of Greek coins were made from silver. It is interesting to note that the actual coinage was supervised by the priests who also used their temples for the storage of the silver.

The exact production methods for early coins remain a mystery. The weights were amazingly consistent although we do not know what methods were taken for standardization. With our limited knowledge of ancient Greek technology, we have not been able to devise an approach to coinage which could match the quality they achieved. The method has been lost.

All coins were crudely struck by hand. It was not until the seventeenth century A.D. that machinery was used to produce coins.

We do know that the metal for the blanks was heated to a liquid, then poured into appropriately sized molds for striking. Exact weight was also determined, although we do not know how it was done.

The dies were made of an alloy of bronze and tin or of iron. The lower die contained the obverse face and was attached to an anvil. The coin blank, heated to make it soft, was placed on the lower die. The upper die was placed on top and struck with a hammer. The blow left both obverse and reverse impressions on the blank, producing a finished coin.

The methods were crude but the workmen quickly became skilled in their craft. Not only were many of the coins quite beautiful, they were also consistent in appearance, the result of an even striking pressure. Only the blanks were noticeably irregular.

The names of the coin designers have been lost. We can guess at their identities by studying the names which occasionally appear on coins. Most of these names refer to Greek leaders rather than coin designers, but a few, which cannot be traced to any other person, are assumed to be the signatures of the artists.

The coin designers were probably selected from among the carvers of gemstones. These craftsmen had been practicing their art for many years prior to the introduction of coins. They worked in a manner similar to that needed to produce a coin and they were accustomed to producing elegant designs on small objects.

The quality of their work is even more remarkable when it is compared with modern coinage. In ancient times the artist worked directly on the actual die used for striking the coins. There was no way to reduce a larger design. Today the artist makes a large model of the coin, correcting any errors and perfecting the design. He then reduces the large model mechanically, making the final coin die flawless.

The art of coinage advanced with the passage of time and today it is a highly sophisticated, mechanized business. But the history of coins and the history depicted by coins has sometimes been dramatic, sometimes humorous, and always interesting as will be shown in the chapters that follow.

2

The Coinage of Augustus

Of all the coins in history, perhaps none are quite as interesting as those of Ancient Rome. Each new portrait coin, for example, was used both to acquaint the people with a ruler's image and to show who was in power at any given moment. The coins have an almost photographic accuracy and include the ruler's every facial flaw, providing us with the most accurate record of the appearance of Roman leaders found in any source. They also reveal the many leadership struggles since the coin designs were altered according to which individual was gaining or losing power in Rome.

The coins served as mini-newspapers, bringing information about wars, architectural triumphs, and other achievements to the inhabitants of the far corners of the Empire. Our knowledge of Roman architecture relies heavily on coinage which shows buildings, many of which fell into ruin centuries ago.

Coins were also used for propaganda purposes. They often contained slogans and sayings meant to promote either an Emperor or one of his pet projects.

Our story of Roman coinage begins with a glimpse of the man considered one of the greatest leaders of antiquity. His name was Gaius Octavius when he was born on September 24, 63 B.C., but he would be better known by the name conferred upon him by the Senate in Rome—Augustus.

Octavius came from a family of wealth and position. His grandfather was a banker and his father was a senator. His mother was the sister of Gaius Julius Caesar, a rising politician who would one day lead Rome This same uncle would later adopt his nephew as a son, insuring the youth's rise to power.

Although Octavius' family was successful, they were not part of the

15

A coin of Augustus (actual size). The bull symbolized the dominating power of Rome over the Empire.

aristocracy which was normally the source of future leaders. Caesar ignored this fact and brought his nephew into elite social circles as he groomed him for power. He even went so far as to arrange for Octavius to preside over some of the summer games.

Caesar later sent Octavius to Macedonia as part of his education. Plans had been made for him to spend the winter at the Greek city of Apollonia, located on the Adriatic Coast south of Dyrrachium. He was to receive advanced military training from officers of the Roman legions stationed nearby as well as studying under the great orator Apollodorus of Pergamum.

Slightly more than three months had passed when his mother sent a freedman with a letter for him. It told of the murder of Caesar by Brutus, Cassius, and others in the Senate House. She wrote that the future was uncertain and asked him to return home at once. There was a chance that the plot was widespread and any relative of Caesar should fear for his life, although this concern proved unfounded.

A few of the centurians felt that Octavius had been given enough training to take control of the military, but he was only 19 and felt that such an effort might end in failure. If that occurred he knew his opposition would kill him.

The people of Apollonia offered Octavius sanctuary but he decided to set sail across the Adriatic at once. He landed 20 miles south of his home to avoid a confrontation with any of the conspirators who might be waiting for him. He walked to the town of Lupiae where he was able to gain more information about his uncle's murder.

The townspeople told him that Marcus Antonius, Caesar's consul, had agreed to grant the murderers amnesty. They also revealed that Caesar's will had been opened and Octavius was named heir to three-fourths of the estate. In addition, he had been formally adopted as the late ruler's son. He took the new name of Gaius Julius Caesar Octavianus.

Octavius realized that what danger he might have been in had passed. In reality there had never been any risk for him. The conspirators did not want a bloodbath. They were high-minded men who had murdered Caesar as the only way they could rid Rome of his tyrannical power, and there had never been any plan to kill Caesar's family or followers.

The death had also proven beneficial to Antony, the surviving consul. He had taken Caesar's papers and money from Calpurnia, Caesar's wife, and had summoned the Senate to a meeting in the temple of Tellus. Although the majority of the men in the Senate were pleased with Caesar's death, Antony persuaded them not to honor the murderers. He realized that many citizens had strongly supported Caesar. He knew that the power of any successor would be weakened if the killers were praised.

Antony impressed the Senators with his call for moderation. He arranged an amnesty for the murderers but sent them from Rome to placate those who wanted revenge. He also secured his personal military power by taking control of the legions in Cisalpine Gaul.

Although Caesar's will favored the young Octavius, Antony quickly became the most powerful man in Rome. He did not see the youth as a threat for he thought the boy was too inexperienced to rally public support.

Antony made a serious mistake in under-rating Octavius. The boy had a spirit which drove him beyond the apparent limits of his frail body. He was to prove a formidable adversary despite his age and physical weakness.

The followers of Caesar soon became divided in their loyalty. Some chose to follow the late ruler's wishes by giving their support to Octavius. The others followed Antony, forcing a showdown which was preceded by Antony's leaving Italy.

Antony took advantage of his friendships to strengthen his forces. Lepidus, Asinius Pollio, and other leaders active in Spain and Gaul brought their legions to assist him.

But violence was not to prove the answer. By November of 43 B.C., Antony, Lepidus, and Octavius met in conference. They agreed that further violence and hostility would be foolish. It was time for them to work together against their common enemies. If they would consolidate their power, they reasoned, they would be invincible.

A coin of Augustus (actual size). The reverse shows Caius and Lucius Caesars standing facing each other, with shields and spears between them.

The three leaders agreed to promote themselves to the role of triumvirs for the next five years. This would give them supreme power over everyone, including the magistrates and senators. They also divided the western provinces among themselves. Antony received Cisalpine and Transalpine Gaul. Lepidus received the two Spains and Octavius received Africa, Sicily, and Sardinia. Octavius and Antony would do battle against the troops of Brutus and Cassius who controlled the east while Lepidus returned to Italy to rule in their absence.

This was the period when the first coinage of Octavius began to appear. A rare gold aureus was struck by the Senate in August of 43 B.C. to commemorate the period when Antony had been forced from Italy. The coin honored Octavius by showing a statue of him which had been erected on the Rostra in the Roman Forum.

The triumvirs began their reign over the country on the first day of the year 42 B.C. They immediately divided up the best land, evicting the people who owned, lived, and worked on it, then giving it to their friends. Large numbers of people were declared enemies for having given support to the murderers of Caesar. Enemy lists were posted and anyone who murdered one of the people named would receive a reward of 25,000 denarii (approximately $5,000) if a free man or 10,000 denarii (approximately $2,000) and his freedom if a slave. The murderers collecting the rewards were also told they would be granted anonymity to prevent reprisals being taken against them.

Prominent citizens suddenly found themselves living in terror, unable to trust family, friends, or servants. Anyone with money or property which might be coveted by the triumvirs knew that any day he could have a bounty placed on his head. Knights and senators fled to the safety of Sicily, but not before more than 2,000 knights and 300 senators were killed.

The planned eastern war was originally going to be financed by selling the land owned by the citizens who had been murdered. This idea
fell through, however, because the people with enough money to buy the
property wanted no part in the bloodletting. They refused to bid on the
stolen land, keeping sale prices very low. The revenue coming in was so
limited that the three leaders were forced to steal land from wealthy
Roman women as well as insisting upon the loan of two percent of all
property owned by anyone having wealth exceeding 100,000 denarii. In
addition, the people making the two percent loan had to donate one
year's income to the war coffers.

In the end, the war was fought and won by the triumvirs. Antony's
military skills brought total victory and the subsequent division of the
eastern provinces.

With the triumvirs working together to lead the people, Antony had
some coins struck showing himself and Octavius as a means of commemorating their harmony. There were also commemorative coins of
necessity which had been ordered struck by military leaders far from
Rome. These necessity coins were unofficial issues which did not have
the approval of the Senate. None of the pieces show much artistic skill as
they were usually produced in areas where die engravers of only limited
ability were working.

Octavius had a sister, Octavia, whose was born in 69 B.C., six years
before him. Her first marriage, in 54 B.C., was to C. Claudius Marcellus,
a man 20 years her senior. They had three children, a son and two
daughters. He died in 40 B.C. and, about the same time, Antony's first
wife, Fulvia, also died. It was decided that in order to solidify relations
between Octavius and Antony, the latter would marry Octavia.

What Octavia may have thought of her forced marriage is not known.
Probably she found her new husband attractive. He was a ladies' man
who, while married to Fulvia, had made Cleopatra, the queen of Egypt,
his mistress. He had had two children by Cleopatra, but Octavia probably looked upon his unfaithfulness as something only of concern to the
late Fulvia rather than herself. It had all happened before the planned
marriage.

In reality, Antony probably would have preferred to wed Cleopatra.
However, he could not legitimately marry a foreigner, so keeping her his
mistress was the best he could hope to do.

Antony ordered the striking of special commemorative coins to celebrate the wedding. On one Octavia is on the reverse, her head atop a

A coin of Augustus (actual size). The reverse legend, within an oak wreath, refers to the increase in public safety which resulted from Augustus' ending of the civil war that had divided Rome.

cylindrical basket and between two snakes. Another coin shows both their heads on the obverse, his being the more prominent to show his dominance. These coins mark the first time any woman had ever been depicted on a Roman coin and elevated Octavia to a position of great prominence in the eyes of the people.

The triumvirate coinage had the distinction of being the first to be reasonably standardized. The coins were mostly made from gold or silver which was carefully weighed so the intrinsic value and the marked value would be extremely close. The coins could serve at full value anywhere in the lands under their control.

Octavius decided to use coins as a way of linking himself with his late uncle in the minds of the people, even though the two men were quite different personalities. Octavius was a poor military tactician and somewhat of a coward in combat. He tried to stay away from the heavy fighting. Battles, such as the one fought in Philippi, were won despite his presence, not because of it. He was bright and cunning with a strong will, but his abilities lay in the civil side of government, not the military. He was never able to adjust to the pressures of combat.

Octavius was one of the few rulers who, during the triumvirate period, allowed only coins which "lied" about his appearance. His features had to be "adjusted" so they appeared similar to those of Caesar's coins. An accurate description of him as he looked during this period can *not* be obtained solely from the study of the coins as it could with other rulers.

Relations among the members of the triumvirate disintegrated to the point that by 32 B.C. it had ceased to exist. Lepidus had been deserted by his men and forced from power four years earlier. Antony, urged on by Cleopatra, was ready for a showdown with Octavius. Each man had established his own government and had large numbers of troops ready for battle.

During this period Antony had further angered Octavius by flaunting his relationship with Cleopatra and honoring her on his coinage. He ordered pieces struck which commemorated his conquest of Armenia in 34 B.C. and his triumphant arrival in Alexandria. The coins bear portraits of Cleopatra and Antony. To make matters worse, this was all done while Antony was still married to Octavia.

In 31 B.C., Antony and Cleopatra mobilized 500 warships, 75,000 foot soldiers, and 12,000 horse soldiers in Greece for an attack against Octavius. Huge grain supplies were brought from Egypt and stockpiled at strategic points throughout Greece. The only flaw in the plan was the timing. The weather was growing cold and it would be difficult to land ships in Italy. It was decided to leave the soldiers in the Gulf of Ambracia on the west coast of Greece throughout the winter. It was to prove a fatal decision.

When Antony first amassed his troops, his forces were far superior to those of Octavius. The latter could not have survived an attack. However, the time delay gave Octavius a chance to raise his own army. By Spring Octavius was able to cross the Adriatic with 80,000 foot soldiers, 12,000 horse soldiers, and 400 ships. His unchallenged action put Antony on the defensive. Worse, the area where Antony's men had been stationed during the winter had not been chosen for its strategic potential. His men were open to blockade and easily cut off from communication. His fleet was isolated and the soldiers were separated from their supplies.

Octavius was victorious without his men ever having to engage in a major battle. The troops Cleopatra had organized were not enthusiastic about going to war so they evaded the blockade and returned to Egypt. The ships of Antony's armada were either sunk, captured, or surrendered without a fight. His troops abandoned their leader and gave up. Antony fled to Alexandria a broken man.

When Octavius at last took full control of the Roman Republic, he discovered that the coinage situation was out of hand. All silver coins were approved by the Senate and their production was fairly well controlled. This was not the case with the gold coins, however. Gold pieces were minted by the generals, a privilege of their rank. They produced the gold pieces with slogans and portraits designed to honor themselves as well as to meet the payroll for the troops.

A coin of Augustus (actual size). The reverse legend refers to Augustus' triumph over Parthia and the return of the Roman military ensign.

To make matters worse, there was no accounting by the generals as to how much gold they had and how many coins they struck. They could sack and plunder a territory without ever revealing the extent of their spoils to the government. In addition they constantly requisitioned money from the treasury. Pompey was the only military leader who ever offered to return to the treasury some of the money taken from plundered cities. Even Pompey only returned 50 million denarii, a small fraction of what the generals were keeping for themselves.

Caesar, for example, had a private debt of 25 million sesterces which he eliminated by starting wars and keeping the booty. His war in Gaul, for example, brought him 400 million sesterces (about 20 million dollars) just from the sale of captives. He produced so many coins that even so intrinsically valuable and generally stable a medium as gold dropped in price by one-sixth its original value. He also took money from the public treasury, including funds to finance his personal vendetta against Pompey in 40 B.C.

When Caesar died, Antony took 175 million denarii from the treasury in order to pay his personal debts. Even Octavius had not been above dipping into the public till. Naturally the treasury had been drastically depleted and new ways of raising revenue had to be found.

Under earlier rulers, the answer had been to tax and assess just about everything. Fees had to be paid for property, slaves, and inheritances. In 44 B.C., for example, a tax of ten asses (at 12-1/2 cents) was imposed on every roof tile in the city. Octavius even went so far as to take 25 percent of the annual income of the cities as well as an additional tax on all freedmen who had 50,000 denarii or more. The latter was to finance his war against Antony. When Octavius finally took complete power, coinage, finance, and taxation were arbitrary and chaotic.

Octavius, as first Emperor of Rome, had to set himself to the task of developing policies which would alter the financial condition of the Empire and help to develop a more stable situation. The public treasury run by the Senate was bankrupt so Octavius generously subsidized it with money from his personal income as well as money taken from some of the older provinces. It seemed that although he may have dipped greedily into the funds while he was a triumvir, when he rose to total command he matured in his thinking, placing concern for the Empire above desire for personal gain.

Next he began the slow process of downgrading the importance of the public treasury, gradually merging it with the imperial treasury which included the emperor's personal wealth. This process would take three centuries to complete, but when one considers the number of years the old system had operated, it might be said that the change occurred overnight.

The coinage of this time was mostly concerned with publicizing Octavius' triumphs. Several pieces show the arch in the Forum and the new temple to Minerva which Octavius had erected to celebrate his victory over Antony and Cleopatra. His title was Imperator on the coins, a word meaning Emperor.

It was also at this time that many of his coins began showing the image of the Egyptian Sphinx, though the reason behind this is not known. Some say it was to symbolize his triumph over the Egyptians. The credibility of this theory is supported by the fact that he must have hated Cleopatra for the liaison with his sister's husband. However, there are several reasons why this theory may not be valid.

After Antony's death, Octavia brought Cleopatra's children, the ones belonging to Antony, to live with her. She raised them with her own children, showing them equal amounts of affection. No matter what her personal feelings, they were obviously not so strong as to embitter the sympathetic Octavius.

Another factor in the mystery is that Octavius had a signet ring made with the design of the Sphinx. This ring was used for sealing both diplomatic and private papers. Whatever his reasons for the symbol's use, the information has been lost to history.

On January 16, 27 B.C., the title "Augustus" was formally conferred on Octavius by a decree of the Senate. The action came three days after laurel trees were placed in front of the door of his house and an oak wreath hung above it. An aureus struck that year commemorated the event, showing an eagle with spread wings, holding an oakwreath in his talons. Two branches of laurel were behind the bird.

Many of the coins struck during this period were commemoratives honoring Augustus for actions improving conditions of the Empire. For example, there were gold and silver pieces telling of his having the highways repaired, especially the Via Flaminia. The later project he planned with his own money, a civic action unknown in the past.

In the next few years the coinage told, among other events, of Augustus' expansion of the Empire. For example, Spain had long been a desired territory, eagerly sought by leaders of the Roman Republic. Numerous armies had invaded the Iberian peninsula, only to be beaten back by the savage inhabitants of Lusitania, Galicia, and Cantabria. Only the southern province of Baetica and a few small eastern coastal towns had ever been captured until Augustus went after the territory between 27 B.C. and 24 B.C. His efforts marked the beginning of the end of Spanish independence. When he left, he ordered Agrippa to continue the struggle. Agrippa was victorious, bringing Spain under Roman rule just five years later. A series of denarii and gold and silver pieces were struck by the coiner P. Carisius to commemorate the events and acquaint the people with the expansion.

Architectural changes were also noted. Coins of 29 B.C. show an arch erected in the Forum Romanum near the Temple of the Divine Julius. Eleven years later, in 18 B.C., the coins show that two additional arches had been added to perpetuate the memory of the recovery of some Roman standards which had been earlier captured by Parthia. The standards were of great symbolic importance to the people and appear numerous times on coinage of this period. The triple arch was just one of many ways the government glorified the return, but knowledge of the structure would have been completely lost were it not for the coins. All that remains today are some marble bases giving no hint of the grandeur of the edifices which once rested on them.

For 17 years, from 20 B.C. until 3 B.C., Augustus granted certain Romans the privilege of striking coins in all metals and putting their names on them. This was apparently a concession to those who still sought some of the conditions which existed when Rome was considered a Republic rather than an Empire. Surprisingly, this privilege was not withdrawn in 15 B.C. when a monetary reform was put into effect. That reform had granted the Senate the right to strike coins of copper and brass while Octavius reserved for himself the right to coin gold and

A coin of Augustus (actual size). The reverse shows the god Apollo holding his lyre. Apollo was the god of health, literature and the arts.

silver. Unfortunately, this power of the Emperor would be abused by later leaders who would drastically debase the metal used for coinage.

By 5 A.D., Augustus had concluded that a separate treasury would be necessary for the financing of the Roman army. The major expenditures of the Empire were for the maintenance, pay, and pensions of the soldiers. It was an expense that had been allowed to grow without being brought under central control.

Augustus was anxious for public support of the new treasury. He decided to start it with 170 million sesterces of his own money, supplementing the funds with a 5 percent inheritance tax and a sales tax.

The public had been overburdened with taxes when the new treasury was started so Augustus decided to try a new approach—indirect taxation. Customs taxes were increased, then the Empire was divided into multiple districts with a tax placed on goods brought across district boundaries or transported from Rome to any of the districts. Additional taxes were placed on inheritances, the slave trade, and other items.

In addition to his other monetary reforms, Augustus centralized the minting of coins. Highly skilled engravers were brought to the capital from all corners of the Empire. They were to produce the most beautiful coins possible, with the pieces destined for use both in Rome and all parts of the country. Provinces might still produce some coins of their own occasionally, but only when there was a severe coin shortage. As a result, Roman coins took on a beauty and consistency of quality that had never been achieved before.

In 14 A.D., when he was 76 years old, Augustus ordered a census taken of the people. He then made a journey to Campania, disregarding his weakened health. As he passed through Nola, returning to Rome from Naples, he became seriously ill and died on August 19. He was ruler with the triumvirate for 12 years and Emperor for 44 years more.

Although he began his career as a tyrant, when Augustus rose in power to become Rome's first Emperor he also matured in wisdom and his sense of humanity. His actions were taken for the betterment of the people and he was able to bring peace to a land that had been torn by internal strife for far too many years.

The system of coinage and taxation Augustus left behind altered the Empire. For the first time in its history, the money of Rome was considered stable enough in value to be used for trade with all the countries of the known world. The intrinsic value of the coins was consistent from piece to piece and the number of gold coins struck was limited to prevent too much of the metal entering circulation.

Augustus also left a special legacy to the people. His will ordered his 1.4 billion sesterce estate divided up with the bulk of his wealth going to the people of Rome. Forty million sesterces were left to the public, 3.5 million to the tribes, 1,000 to each member of the guards, 500 to each man in the city battalions, and 300 to each member of the legions. Only 150 million sesterces were left to blood relations. The people had made him wealthy so he returned his wealth to the people.

3

The Coinage of Nero
and Agrippina

Nero, the arch-villain of antiquity, has the distinction of having what is perhaps the most interesting and colorful coinage of all the major emperors. His life, together with the story of the rise and fall of his mother, Agrippina, has been well documented in gold, silver, and bronze, which tell, at least in part, of his violence, depravity, and preference for illicit sex.

Nero rose to power mostly because of the qualities of his ancestors. His great-great-grandfather was Augustus, the founder of the Roman Empire and one of its most beloved leaders. Just 40 years before Nero came to power, Augustus died and was declared a god of Rome. Augustus was the leader who managed to defeat Antony and Cleopatra, took control of a society covering most of the Mediterranean region, and ended the constant civil wars and united the people.

Nero's mother, Agrippina, was born in 15 A.D. and was just four years old when her father died in Syria. The Emperor Tiberius was in power and he was an enemy of the family. He had Agrippina's mother arrested when the girl was 14. The woman was exiled to an island where she was beaten so badly that she lost one of her eyes. The Emperor planned to continually torture and humiliate her, but she prevented this by deliberately starving to death.

Other members of the family met equally tragic fates. One of Agrippina's brothers was taken to an island after being arrested on a charge of homosexuality. He died by his own hand after being given a choice between execution and suicide.

A second brother was placed in a dungeon where he was subjected to torture and starvation so severe that he tried to eat the stuffing of his mattress. He was driven insane before his death.

Only one of Agrippina's brothers, Caligula, survived the reign of terror. He took control of the empire a few years later.

As was normal for a girl in ancient Rome, Agrippina became engaged at the age of 13. The man was Cnaeus Domitius Ahenobarbus, about whom no one ever spoke a kind word. Once, as he was riding in his chariot along the Appian Way, he spotted a young boy in the road. He killed the youth by deliberately running him down. He was even incapable of relaxing without violence. He killed a man who refused to drink with him and gouged out the eye of an unfortunate with whom he got in an argument.

Nero's father seemed to recognize his personal shortcomings. On the birth of his son Lucius Domitius, later known as Nero, he commented that "any child of Agrippina and himself must be a loathsome object and a public disaster," according to one writer.

Nero's father was as dishonest as he was violent. Chariot races were a popular pastime in Rome, with the victors winning a palm and substantial sums of money. At one point, Cnaeus was named praetor or magistrate of the games, an ideal position for his greed. He held back a portion of the prize money for himself, an action which caused protests from everyone else involved in the races.

Cnaeus was charged with treason, incest, and adultery by Tiberius, who ordered his execution. But Tiberius died on March 16, 37 A.D., before the sentence could be carried out. Two days later, Agrippina's brother Caligula rose to power, and spared the life of his brother-in-law. Cnaeus only lived three more years, though, succumbing to dropsy when Nero was 14.

Agrippina was delighted with her brother's action. So delighted, in fact, that she joined her sisters in sharing the new Emperor's bed.

Caligula's incest was in keeping with his character. He felt so warmly towards his sisters that he had earlier named them "Honorary Vestal Virgins." That action was taken at a time when they were all married and when Agrippina was pregnant with Nero.

Agrippina's new prominence in court triggered her lust for power. She and her sisters were honored in all oaths and vows. In addition, the Senate authorized the striking of a brass coin showing the three sisters in symbolic poses. Agrippina, leaning against a column, represented Security. Her two sisters represented Fortuna and Concordia.

A coin of Nero (actual size). The reverse shows the Goddess of Concord. According to beliefs of the time, it was important to worship her because through her small things became great.

The year before Cnaeus' death, Agrippina had taken a lover, who was later accused of plotting against Caligula. The outraged Caligula had the lover put to death, his body cremated, and his ashes saved. He forced his sister to carry the ashes from Moguntiacum to Rome in mockery of the pilgrimage Agrippina's mother had made carrying the ashes of the beloved Germanicus. She was then ordered into exile.

Cnaeus was understandably displeased with his wife's actions. When he died, two-thirds of his estate was inherited by Caligula, the rest going to the infant Nero. But with Agrippina temporarily in exile, there was no one to speak for the baby. Caligula took the entire inheritance, leaving Nero in the care of Domitia Lepida, Cnaeus' sister. The aunt did not want Nero, especially since his inheritance was gone. She kept him in squalor, cared for by a male dancer and a barber.

Agrippina returned from exile after Caligula's death in 41 A.D. She saw to it that her son's inheritance was restored, then increased his wealth by marrying the wealthy orator Crispus Passienus. This was not one of the orator's wiser moves. As soon as Agrippina was certain of the additional inheritance, she helped her husband reach his unnatural death in 44 A.D.

The new emperor, Claudius, was married to Messalina, a jealous woman who looked upon the young Nero as a rival for her husband's affection. She became so enraged that she gave orders to have the child smothered in his bed while he slept, a fate he narrowly escaped. Messalina later committed suicide, supposedly the result of a deranged state of mind. However, the reason was more likely that her husband had learned about a wild party Messalina had given in his absence. Among those in attendance was her lover, a man whom she hoped to put on the throne.

No matter how poor a mother Agrippina may have been, she did want to prepare her son for leadership. She chose Seneca, the great philosopher and teacher, to act as tutor for the young Nero. The boy, considered quiet, kind, and eager to learn, soon found delight in the praise he received for his singing, dancing, and playing of the pipes. He learned public speaking and seemed to have a talent for the theater. Exactly how skilled he may have been is not known: before he became Emperor he was not important enough for written records to have been kept of his performances, while after he became Emperor there was unanimous agreement that he was more talented than anyone had ever been before. This may have been the result of his great ability or, more likely, because any adverse comments about the Emperor would result in the critic's death.

The widower Claudius felt he should have a new wife and the choice fell upon his niece, Agrippina. Supposedly his decision was made based on the advice of his Greek finance minister, who said that the union would link the two families of Augustus. However, Agrippina had been secretly scheming to become his wife in order to enhance her power. She had earlier taken one of Claudius' close advisers as her lover in order to exert some influence over her uncle. But as soon as the older man began showing her some attention, she disposed of her lover and concentrated on becoming the wife of the Emperor.

At this point Roman coinage begins to document the rise to power of Agrippina and her son Nero. Claudius was a weak man when it came to women. He was easily swayed by their influence and desires. The power-mad Agrippina, just 34 years old, recognized her husband's failings and took advantage of them. She was able to use her influence to rapidly take control of the government.

Agrippina was intelligent in her maneuvering for power. The public had hated Messalina, falsely accusing her of trying to run the Empire. But Agrippina's public appearances gave no hint of her greed. The public trusted and loved her, despite the fact that she was guilty of all the charges that had been brought against her predecessor.

Around 50 A.D. gold and silver coins bearing Agrippina's portrait began appearing throughout the Empire. These show her with the title AUGUSTA, a title which implies leadership of the Empire, an amazing situation. All the emperors were known as Augustus, but even the first Augustus' wife, a woman who had been greatly loved by the people, did not presume to elevate herself to the level of power that the name Augusta

A coin of Nero (actual size). The reverse shows a triumphal arch and, above it, soldiers running, bearing trophies. It was erected in 62 A.D. to celebrate victory over Parthia. Later it was learned that the armies had actually met with disaster, but the arch was completed anyway.

indicated. These coins reveal that Agrippina was considered the equal of her husband, a fact made even more extraordinary when you consider that the Roman constitution did not allow for an empress.

The early portraits of Agrippina are serious and cold, giving no hint of her lustful passions. When both she and her husband are depicted on the same side, she is in the background, with only her eye, forehead, nose, and mouth visible. This indicated that although they were supposedly equal rulers, he was the dominant leader—at least in the public eye.

Agrippina knew she could never take sole command of the empire and her control over her husband was less than she desired. To make matters worse, Claudius had a natural son, Britannicus, who was both four years younger than Nero and technically the rightful heir.

The first step in eliminating the threat of Britannicus was to have Nero become engaged to Octavia, Claudius' natural daughter. The marriage was scheduled for four or five years in the future but the engagement increased his power with the government.

The engagement violated one of the rules for society set by the original Augustus and strictly followed by all succeeding rulers. According to Augustus, a girl could not become engaged until she was ten, nor married until she was twelve. Since Octavia was only nine, it was obvious that Agrippina had great influence over her husband in order to gain his permission for the betrothal.

Technically, it was the girl's second engagement. When she was a year old she had been promised to another youth, although this was an engagement made for political reasons. This first fiancé committed suicide after Agrippina arranged for him to be framed on a charge of incest. She took this action before she had married Claudius, a fact which shows how long she had been planning to take control of the Empire.

Nero was formally adopted by Claudius on February 25, 50 A.D. This was an unusual action but Agrippina informed her husband that the precedent had been set by Augustus who had adopted his stepson Tiberius. What Agrippina shrewdly did not mention was the fact that Tiberius had succeeded his stepfather on the throne, another precedent she wanted Nero to follow.

A year later Nero was admitted to the Equestrian Order with the title Princeps Juventutis. The coins that were struck to honor this occasion made it evident that Nero was destined to eventually take control of the Empire as heir to Claudius.

There were other changes following the adoption. The young Nero, who had been known as Lucius Domitius Ahenobarbus, received a surname common to the Claudian House. He became Tiberius Claudius Nero and later Nero Claudius Caesar Drusus Germanicus.

As Nero rose in power, Brittanicus saw his own position weaken. No official coinage bore his name or portrait and the tutor who had been preparing him for a life of leadership was put to death.

The importance of the coinage must be stressed at this point. Communication between the Emperor in Rome and people in far-off cities under his control was extremely limited. Rising politicians hoping to gain favor with Rome were always uncertain as to the action they should take in regard to the royal family. Plots and counterplots were the norm so it was important not to become connected with a family member whose power was declining. The only way they had to determine the Roman leaders of importance was by studying the coins. The portraits and inscriptions they bore were accurate guides to what was happening in Rome, a city thousands of miles away.

The provincial leaders realized that Nero had gained great power, since his coin portraits were so prominent, and their future relied on his support. They immediately began producing their own coinage bearing his youthful head.

A few politicians decided to cover all possibilities. The governor of Judaea produced coins with the heads of both of Claudius' sons. The governor of Moesia at first issued a brass sestertius with a Latin inscription honoring Nero. Then, thinking he had better promote both sides, he issued a companion piece honoring Britannicus.

Nero's honors came as rapidly as his mother could arrange them. He was legally declared an adult before he had reached his fourteenth birthday. He was made consul or proconsul in various areas outside Rome and allowed to march at the head of the Praetorian guard.

By this time Claudius was degenerating from old age. He was in his sixties, an extremely old age for the time. He was both partially senile and frequently drunk. His temper was violent and unpredictable. To make matters worse for the people, Agrippina had become mentally unbalanced in her drive for power. She began to see plots and intrigues all around her. Of the several hundred soldiers and 30 senators who were murdered by order of the Emperor Claudius, the vast majority were put to death through the efforts of Agrippina during the short period in which she was married to her uncle.

Agrippina relied on the people's belief in astrology and magic to rid herself of many of her real and imagined enemies. One of her victims was Domitia Lepida, Nero's aunt, whom Agrippina saw as a major rival. Both wanted to guide Nero's life and each considered herself the most prominent woman in Rome.

Domitia Lepida was accused of using magic to do away with Agrippina. Claudius was the judge at her trial and Nero, then 17, lied in order to provide the most damaging testimony. The verdict was death.

Agrippina gradually reached a point where friend and enemy became confused in her mind. One of her most devoted informers was ordered expelled from the senate. She had violent temper tantrums which so upset Claudius that he hinted she could be exiled like her mother if she did not calm down. Such threats were not to be taken lightly so Agrippina decided it was time to do away with her husband and take control of the Empire through her son.

No one knows exactly how Claudius died. A case could be made for natural causes. He was old and not very well. However, it is far more likely that Agrippina arranged for him to meet his end.

One story says that Agrippina tried to poison her husband. She supposedly went to a convicted woman poisoner and asked her to prepare a meal for the Emperor. Or, if other writers are correct, she merely obtained some poison which she sprinkled on his meal. Whatever the case, Claudius was supposedly so drunk by the time he ate the tainted dinner that the poison did not take effect rapidly enough to kill him. The bulk of the poison passed through his body and was eliminated with his normal waste.

Coins of Nero (actual size). The reverses show Ceres sitting with corn ears in her right hand, a torch in her left. Opposite to her is the Goddess of Plenty, Annona. The coins were meant to show Nero's generosity in sharing food with the people.

Agrippina then enlisted the aid of Rome's leading doctor, Stertinius Xenophon of Cos, a man whose greed matched his medical knowledge. He felt that the risks of being part of a plot against the Emperor were offset by the rewards to be gained if the plot was successful. He told the Emperor that he needed to make him vomit. This was accomplished by tickling his throat with a feather that just happened to have been tipped in a fast-acting poison. Death was swift and Nero took the throne on October 13, 54 A.D.

Agrippina played the role of the grieving widow, deeply moving all those who did not know the truth. Under Roman custom, deceased rulers could be declared gods and the ruler's widow could be the one to propose deification. In one of her few acts of charity, Agrippina ordered her husband deified. She followed this action by becoming the priestess of the Divine Claudius and ordered a temple built in his honor. A magnificent series of coins was produced, each showing the late ruler's head and the inscription DIVVS CLAVDIVS AVGVSTVS.

Additional coins appeared the following year. One piece showed the images of both Claudius and Augustus, each declared a god after his death, seated in an elephant-drawn chariot. Their heads are crowned with sun rays and around the edge of the coins are Agrippina's name and titles.

Agrippina had finally taken control of the Empire. Her power was evident in the official coinage of Rome. The gold and silver pieces showed the heads of Nero and his mother facing each other. Although both their names and titles appear on the coins, Agrippina's name appears on the obverse, near their portraits. Nero's name is on the reverse, meaning that the coins were meant to honor Agrippina. They would relay to the people the message that Rome's leader was a woman. All references to her on the coin are in the language reserved for the Emperor. It can honestly be said that, at the moment, she was the most important person in the Roman Empire.

By the following year Nero had begun to gain the upper hand to some degree. Coins generally showed Nero and Agrippina in profile, side by side, in much the same manner as she had appeared on her late husband's coinage. Nero's name was on the obverse and Agrippina, mentioned as "Augusta, mother of the Augustus," on the reverse. At least one coin, a silver piece from Caesarea, put Agrippina's portrait on the reverse as well.

Whatever good qualities Nero might have had as a child, Nero the man was repugnant to behold. He suffered from "spots and body odor," according to one writer. "His hair was light blond, his features fine rather than attractive, his eyes bluish grey and rather weak, his neck too thick, his stomach protuberant, and his legs very thin." He also had a tendency to squint from nearsightedness.

Despite Nero's physical shortcomings, the fact that he was Emperor made him highly desirable to woman. Agrippina was getting older and knew her influence was waning. Her son had married Octavia and no longer paid close attention to her wishes.

Agrippina tried sex and blackmail to control her son. First she would get him drunk, then seduce him into an incestuous relationship. When he began to tire of this she told him that he had to follow her wishes or she would support Britannicus as the rightful heir to the throne.

The existence of Britannicus frightened Nero. Although the youth was only 14 and too young to rule, he was the rightful heir of Claudius. To make matters worse, leaders in some of the provinces thought that

Nero might have to be forced to step down in favor of his step-brother. For example, coins were issued in Hippo Diarrhytus featuring Britannicus. The leaders who authorized these coins were stripped of power by an angry Nero, and a few of them were murdered.

Nero then went to Britannicus' tutors and arranged for them to poison the youth. However, the initial attempt failed because the poison was too weak.

Failure was tolerated once but the tutors faced death if they did not succeed with their second attempt. The tutors gathered at the palace and, in front of the Emperor, prepared a second, more lethal dose.

The poison was cleverly administered during a banquet. Warm wine was given to the prince, who turned it over to the official taster. The wine was harmless, but when the taster returned it to Britannicus, the youth thought it was too hot. Following the custom of the day, a few drops of water were added to cool it. It was in the water that the poison had been hidden. When Britannicus took a second taste he had violent convulsions and died at the table.

The guests were horrified by the sight of the writhing youth, but Nero was quick to assure them that everything was perfectly normal. He explained that his step-brother was subject to epileptic fits, and that what was happening was not serious and the youth would recover shortly. He failed to mention either the poison or the fact that before the banquet he had made arrangements for the cremation of his brother's body.

The royal physicians had limited medical knowledge but Nero feared there was a chance they could save Britannicus. He ordered everyone to stay away from the body until he was certain all life had passed from it. Then he had the boy removed and cremated immediately—just in case.

The death of Britannicus eliminated any chance for Agrippina to blackmail her son. To make matters worse for Agrippina, Nero took on a mistress, Claudia Acte. She was a freewoman who had originally been a slave from Asia. His mother condoned this relationship at first, hoping to retain some influence through friendship. But after a while she spoke out in favor of her daughter-in-law, whom the Emperor had grown to hate. Agrippina was ordered to move from the palace for her efforts.

By 55 A.D. Roman coinage shows that Agrippina had lost all of her power. Her position as Priestess of the Divine Claudius had lost all meaning, and her head was removed from official and provincial coinage. Coins and inscriptions relating to Claudius were almost entirely

A coin of Nero (actual size). The reverse shows Nero, bareheaded and holding a spear, accompanied by another warrior. It celebrated the cavalry maneuvers of the pretorian soldiers.

eliminated and Nero even went so far as to erect a statue in memory of his real father.

Agrippina was allowed to reside in a mansion away from the palace but her drop from power was emphasized by the removal of the military escort which had followed her for years. On the occasions when Nero visited her he always went in the company of staff officers. He would embrace her for a moment, then leave. It was the least he felt he owed her but she would get nothing more.

With Agrippina fallen from power, Nero began to feel the strain of ruling alone. He decided he needed new ways to relax and periodically escape the problems of government. Although he enjoyed the theater, he often found the greatest pleasure in watching the fights of the street gangs who seemed to perpetually argue about the qualities of various male dancers. The intensity of feeling was so great that the arguments would degenerate into violence that could only be stopped by soldiers who patrolled the streets.

Nero knew it was beneath his dignity as Emperor to join in the violence but he was tired of being an observer at the street battles. He decided to wear a wig, disguise his identity, and venture forth at night, beating up passers-by and taking sexual liberties with both women and boys. He used the element of surprise to gain the upper hand, although after one of his victims resisted him, he became so frightened that he ordered loyal, tough soldiers to accompany him. They were out of uniform and served the sole purpose of keeping anyone from interfering with the Emperor's "fun."

If anyone recognized the empire's leader, he kept the knowledge to himself. Only a senator, Montanus, dared to admit he knew the identity of his attacker. He made the mistake of defending himself, then apologized to Nero when he realized who his assailant had been.

Nero was upset by the chance that his brutality would be exposed. He informed the senator that a convenient suicide would be in order. Montanus knew the alternative was probably death by torture and decided that suicide would be far less painful.

There is a good chance that the people of Rome knew their Emperor was a bully. They were certain that he condoned the rising street violence and there may have been a few who secretly knew he was involved, but none of them ever publicly admitted such thoughts.

Agrippina's influence ended permanently as the result of Nero's taking on a new mistress. Her name was Poppaea Sabina, a woman of great beauty, intelligence, and an unprincipled ambition that was possibly as strong as Agrippina's.

Poppaea Sabina was born in 31 A.D. Her mother had been driven to suicide by Messalina, the wife of Claudius whom Agrippina had worked to destroy. The woman's offence had been to fall in love with Mnester, the pantomime actor who was also Messalina's lover.

Nero's mistress was first married in 44 A.D. to Rufrius Crispinus, a knight who served as prefect of the praetorian guard. He was an undistinguished soldier who was displaced in his command 7 years later at the whim of Agrippina.

Poppaea Sabina had her first recorded affair in 58 A.D. when she met M. Salvius Otho, 26 years old, was blissfully happy. He praised his bride to all who would listen, his words reaching the ears of Nero who asked to meet such a beautiful young woman. Soon she was the Emperor's mistress.

Some of the early writers were rather extreme in their attitude towards the new woman in Nero's life. Tacitus described her, in part, by saying, "She had every asset except goodness. From her mother, the loveliest woman of her day, she inherited distinction and beauty. Her wealth, too, was equal to her birth. She was clever and pleasant to talk to. She seemed respectable. But her life was depraved. Her public appearances were few; she would half-veil her face at them, to stimulate curiosity (or because it suited her). To her, married or bachelor bedfellows were alike. She was indifferent to her reputation—yet insensible to men's love, and herself unloving. Advantage dictated the bestowal of her favors."

In reality Poppaea Sabina was not so bad as pictured. She had a lust for power which caused her to go with Nero but neither the Emperor nor her husband ever stopped loving her. She was extremely beautiful and so concerned about her appearance that a herd of 500 wild asses was maintained to keep her well supplied with milk for bathing. Her interests were broad and included among other things, an unusual appreciation of the Jewish religion.

Under his new mistress' influence, Nero decided to rid himself of Agrippina once and for all. His first attempt on her life was during the annual festival of the Goddess Minerva, which Nero regularly attended. He asked his mother to join him and sent a boat to take her to and from Baiae where she was to have dinner with her son.

The return trip was to be made on a specially constructed collapsible barge. When the rowers had pulled the boat a sufficient distance from the land, the canopy over Agrippina and her ladies in waiting suddenly collapsed. Heavy pieces of lead crashed down on top, crushing one of the attendants. Then bolts were removed and the vessel was supposed to collapse, but the mechanism proved faulty. The soldiers on board rushed to the side of the boat, hoping to overturn or sink it in order to carry out Nero's orders. They managed to dump Agrippina and her attendants into the water, but she was not killed.

The collapsing boat was so unusual that none of the attendants realized it was a death plot. Acerronia, one of the women on board, thought she would be rescued from the water faster if she called to the men on the boat and told them she was Agrippina. For her efforts she was beaten to death with oars, an act witnessed by Agrippina who wisely stayed silent, swimming to a rescue boat without identifying herself.

Although Nero's mother had fallen from power, the coins bearing her image were still widely circulated. New coins had not been struck for her in several years, but that was a distinction noted only by the government leaders. The average man-on-the-street felt she was still someone to revere. Huge crowds rushed to her villa after the "accident," hoping to see her and let her know they were happy about her escape.

The frustrated Nero sent soldiers to disperse the crowds, then dispatched three trusted aides to pay their "respects." The aides, Anicetus and two naval officers, repeatedly stabbed the old woman, tossed the body on the dining room couch and immediately cremated her.

Nero ignored the public outrage at Agrippina's death. He knew that no one dared accuse him of murder directly and he was deaf to expressions of general displeasure.

He began to feel a new freedom in his life which he celebrated by inaugurating the Ludi Quinquennales, collectively known as the Neronia. These were a series of horse, musical, and gymnastic competitions in imitation of the Greek games. They were promoted and commemorated through a series of copper and brass semisses struck by the Rome mint. The coins all bore the legend, usually abbreviated, "Certamen quinquennale Romae Constitutum."

During the next two to three years Nero took great pride in promotion of architectural triumphs. One series of sestertii commemorates Nero's Triumphal Arch. The arch, which was erected on Capitoline hill by decree of the Senate, commemorated Nero's victories over Parthia. It is interesting to note that without the coins, our only knowledge of this arch would come from the writings of Tacitus. Its physical appearance would have been lost.

In 63 A.D., the year after the coins commemorating the arch appear to have been struck, Nero issued coins showing the Temple of Janus with its doors closed to commemorate the fact that there was finally peace throughout the Empire.

Now we come to the event which forced Nero to change Roman coinage as a means of regaining the support of the people. This was the fire which broke out on July 19, 64 A.D., leaving two-thirds of Rome in ruins.

The basic design of Rome made it highly susceptible to disaster. The people lived crowded together in wooden buildings built almost flush against each other. The eastern end of the Circus Maximus, where the fire first broke out, had a mass of wooden booths filled with combustible articles leaning against the outer walls. A group of men worked as night watchmen to try and spot fires when they first started since even a minor blaze generally destroyed an entire block of the flimsy dwellings. But they were unsuccessful on that awful day in July.

The fire started in wooden structures near the valley between the Palatine and Caelian hills. The fire worked in two directions at the corner of the Palatine, the flames followed the wind currents of the valley. By the time the blaze reached the massive brick temples, the inferno had reached such intensity that instead of stopping the fire, the bricks and stones crumbled in the heat.

The blaze spread uncontrollably. When it seemed to be dying in one area, new parts of the city suddenly erupted into flames. For a week it burned out of control. When it began to burn itself out, three of the 14 regions of Rome were totally destroyed and seven others had been severely damaged. Only four sections remained as they had once been. Countless temples, monuments, and public buildings were reduced to ashes.

Families were made homeless by the fire and prisoners and slaves escaped in the confusion. A few were caught thrusting burning wood into homes and buildings not yet ablaze. They were acting to increase the hysteria while attempting escape. However, when caught they lied and said they were under specific orders from an unnamed authority.

These false confessions were all the public needed to further turn against Nero. He must be the cause of the fire, they reasoned. Rumors began circulating that he had set the blaze, then gone to the Tower of Maecenas to enjoy the spectacle while singing an original song entitled "Sack of Troy." Early historians cried out against the Emperor although they could offer no proof that he was ever involved. In fact, there is ample reason to believe he had nothing to do with the disaster.

Nero was in Antium when the fires began, rushing home as soon as the news reached him. The thousands of homeless Romans were offered shelter in his own imperial gardens as well as in all public buildings that had not burned. He contributed money and other items to the victims, erected temporary living quarters in the Campus Martius, and reduced the price of grain to just three sesterces a modius. A sestertius was equal to approximately 6 cents, so the selling price was thus roughly 18 cents a peck.

There was another reason why the public was suspicious of Nero. He liked to think of himself as a great entertainer and often performed in public. He received rave reviews since criticism meant death. He also had an extremely loyal audience—the result of a rule that no one was allowed to leave during one of his performances. This meant that periodically a baby would be born during his appearances. He also had a rule demanding complete silence. Anyone having an uncontrollable coughing fit could be put to death.

Nero strived for realism during his performances. One of these, the reenactment of the burning of Troy, was "enhanced" by his ordering 12 fires to be set in various parts of Rome in order to create the right mood for the show. The fires were kept under control, but it was a stupid act, callously disregarding the potential public danger. The people felt the flames which destroyed Rome could easily have started as one of his stunts.

Even his efforts to rebuild Rome after the fire brought Nero criticism. He decided that the city should be the most beautiful in the world. He erected an elaborate palace and ornate, costly buildings, statues, and parks. These were all, in effect, monuments to his name. Everyone knew of his great ego so this seemed to be just additional evidence that he was somehow responsible for the fire. After all, the buildings which burned had mostly been dedicated to other rulers.

Nero took two steps to redeem himself with the public. The first was to persecute the Christians and try to blame them for the blaze. This action, of no concern in this chapter, was probably encouraged by his mistress.

Nero also altered the coinage, introducing the artistic quality that had not been seen since the best of the Greek pieces. Many of the coins are miniature masterpieces revealing the highest level of the engraver's art.

The artists who produced the Emperor's portraits for the coins shifted from the totally realistic approach of the past to an idealized type of design. Nero's face was accurately portrayed but the rest of the figure was in the style of the mighty Greek leaders.

It is interesting to note that the portraits show his hair style to be a series of waving curls with points lying flat along his brow. This was the style adopted by members of street gangs and its use on the coins shocked the public. It was the same as if the official portrait of the President of the United States showed him with shoulder length hair, sandals, torn jeans, and a sweatshirt.

The way in which the coins served as propaganda can be seen in the pieces depicting Annona and Ceres, the goddesses of the food supply. Corn was a staple and the annual crop was a major concern. The coins were to serve as a constant reminder to the people that the Emperor was aware of the critical food shortages and was always doing what he could to alleviate the suffering of the people. The seated Ceres holds a torch and ears of corn while Annona, personification of the grain harvest, stands in front of her. The stern of a ship adorned with a garland is in the distance.

A different coin, a brass sestertius, showed Ostia, the chief grain harbor which had been started by Claudius and completed by Nero. On the reverse is Neptune reclining beneath a crescent shaped moon and a row of breakwaters. A statue representing a lighthouse is also on the coin.

The beautiful warrior-goddess Minerva appears on a brass coin. The design was symbolic of the rebuilding of the city and was used to keep the minds of the people on the construction in Rome rather than on the destruction which made rebuilding necessary.

A private issue token honoring Nero has a detailed image of Apollo playing the lyre. It symbolized the Emperor's musical endeavors, implying that they were divine in origin. The tokens are considered private issue rather than legal coins because they lack the marking SC which meant "By a decree of the Senate." However, references to Apollo also appear on Nero's coins. They take the form of the sun-ray crown which so frequently encircles the engraving of Nero's forehead.

Many of the coins depict Nero as a great warrior, something which was quite the opposite of the truth. Nero won his victories through diplomacy, a sign of weakness to the people. As a result, there are coins showing him addressing the troops and others showing him exercising with the Praetorian Guards, two activities in which he did not engage.

Nero also identified with Augustus on the coins. The coins issued on the fiftieth anniversary of Augustus' death show Victory with a shield dedicated to the Emperor by the Senate and Roman People (SPQR). It was symbolic of the Shield of Valor which the Senate and people had dedicated to Augustus. The coinage was meant to imply that Nero was a worthy successor to the late leader.

In 63 A.D. Nero made Poppaea Sabina his second wife. Octavia had been banished from the palace but was still married to Nero. This was something Poppaea found intolerable. She accused Octavia of adultery with a slave, using as proof the testimony of Octavia's maids who gave evidence only after they were tortured.

The charge of adultery meant a slow legal battle and Poppaea was impatient to be rid of her rival. She finally had the soldiers seize Octavia, bind her and cut her veins. When Octavia fainted but failed to bleed to death, she was drowned in a bath, her head severed and carried like a trophy to Nero's wife.

By 66 A.D. Nero had grown tired of Poppaea and frequently argued with her. One domestic quarrel came to blows. He kicked her so hard that she died almost immediately. Ironically, he had granted her wish that she not outlive her beauty.

Despite the apparent passions of the Nero-Poppaea love affair, the coins depicting her are relatively limited. Most of the ones honoring the couple were produced in provinces such as Egypt.

Although Nero was making his coins more beautiful than ever before, he was also making them intrinsically less valuable. By strict definition he was the world's first large-scale counterfeiter. The coinage was represented to be of legally set values when, in fact, it was worth far less than marked.

It had long been a practice of Roman Emperors to squeeze a little extra mileage from their coinage by making them very slightly undervalued in terms of metallic worth. But Nero, faced with the rising cost of rebuilding Rome, felt he had to make the coins stretch farther. Since he personally owned most of the sources for gold and silver, the more coins which could be made from a pound of precious metal, the greater his personal profits.

For example, since the time of Augustus the gold aureus, approximately equal in value to the five dollar gold piece familiar to Americans, had weighed 1/42 of a pound. Nero reduced the weight to 1/45 of a pound. The silver denarius went from 1/84 pound to 1/96 pound, and the alloy in the silver coins was raised from 5 to 10 percent.

Base metal token coinages of copper and brass had existed for years. Their marked values never equalled their intrinsic worth, but the red and golden colors of the coins were popular with the people who enjoyed their beauty. Nero decided to tamper with them by producing only brass coins, the result of his owning the zinc which would be used. The people hated the change so the idea was dropped. To prevent their further wrath he had his best designers work on the copper and brass pieces which were produced in the western mint of Lugdunum as well as in Rome, making them among the most beautiful of his coins.

The debasement of the coinage meant little to the public. They accepted the coins at face value, knowing that merchants would receive them in like measure. There was no hoarding of earlier issues or similar financial reaction.

The only people who were angered by the debasement were those from outside the Empire, such as the Germans. They often hoarded coins of other lands as a means of protecting their savings. They were so outraged that they refused to accept any coins of Nero dated from 64 A.D. onward, though keeping all the coins of his predecessors.

By 68 A.D. the people of Rome and their leaders in the Senate had had enough of Nero. For fourteen years the Empire had been ruled by a man motivated by selfishness and cruelty. Civil war broke out. Julius Vindex gathered 100,000 men in Southern Gaul and convinced Sulpicius Calba, commander of the legions in Spain, to proclaim himself general of the State and Roman people. This was followed by Clodius Macer, commander of the Third Legion in Numidia, who severed alliance with Nero and proclaimed himself Propraetor of Africa.

Finally the Senate ruled Nero to be an enemy of mankind, sentencing him to death in the "traditional" manner. The traditional manner meant that his head would be forced into a wooden fork, then his body whipped until he died. Nero, however, had no intentions of enduring such a fate. He committed suicide by falling on his sword.

For numismatists the horror of the man is just a fascinating sidelight. He was a tyrant and a counterfeiter, but in his coinage there remains a beauty that assures him immortality as much as the tales of his deeds of horror.

4

The Colonial Coinage of John Hull

Everyone knows about the American Revolutionary War of 1776, but few people are aware that one of the first overt acts of rebellion concerned coinage in the Massachusetts Bay Colony. The date was May 27, 1652—more than a century before the war began. This was the date when the first Mint—an illegal one—was established in the British colonies.

Today, Boston, Massachusetts, is a thriving American city that is home to hundreds of thousands of people; in 1652, Boston was a quiet village with approximately 2,000 residents. The houses were built of wood and located along a maze of crooked, unnamed streets. It was a confusing area in which to be a stranger, since one could easily become lost.

The Puritan Community was not a democratic one. The people followed the teachings of John Cotton who wrote, in 1636, that: "Democracy I do not conceive that ever God did ordain as a fit government either for church or commonwealth. If the people be governor who shall be governed? As for monarchy and aristocracy they are both of them clearly approved and directed in Scripture."

Land ownership supported the idea of an aristocracy. The white men had decided that all Massachusetts land belonged to the Massachusetts Bay Company, the Puritan group that had organized the settlement of the colony. The land was broken up and given away, without charge, to groups of settlers who promised to establish new townships. These settlers, known as proprietors, divided their holdings, giving parcels of land to "reputable" persons who were interested in becoming permanent residents of the community. Later on the land would be auctioned instead of donated. The change caused many people to engage in wild speculation, hoping to resell the land they bought at great profit.

Boston society was clearly divided along economic lines. The aristocrats were known as freemen. They were active members of the Puritan Church, law abiding, industrious, and, most important of all, they had money or property worth at least 200 pounds in British money. Such prosperity earned a man many special privileges—including the right to vote. The law was softened in 1691, when the revised Charter dropped the Puritan Church membership requirement and reduced the necessary money holding to 40 pounds sterling.

A freeman was addressed as "Mister" while the average citizen was known as "Goodman" or "Goodwoman"—"Goody" for short. There were so few freemen that only 1,100 existed in the entire state of Massachusetts in the year 1670, a year which saw a total population of approximately 25,000. Even under the revised Charter of 1691, only one-fifth of the adult males qualified.

The Puritans governed themselves strictly during the early years of the Colony. The fees for all commercial transactions as well as the amount of wages which could be paid for various services were all tightly controlled.

A skilled worker was paid two shillings a day, or fourteen pence a day if he received free room and board from his employer. Unskilled workmen received 1-1/2 shillings. An apprentice worked seven years without pay, although most employers gave the young apprentices periodic gifts of money which they were free to spend as they chose. Gifts of larger sums of money were often donated to favored employees since raises in pay were forbidden. Thus a man might earn his two shillings a day and also receive another six shillings a week as a "gift." Even if the gift was given every week, year in and year out, it still did not violate the wage law.

Every able-bodied man in the colony had to work. There was an extremely severe law against idleness. If a man was caught lingering in a tavern for more than an hour during a work day, he was fined 2½ shillings. A second offender was whipped. A third offender was whipped as he ran to the limits of the town, then turned over to the authorities in the next town who continued the whipping through their community, turning him over to the next town and so on, presumably until he was dead, had left the colony, or agreed to work.

Prices seemed to be at two extremes. Food was usually low in cost. A forty pound turkey generally sold for two shillings; a small bird for half that much. A tavern charged two pence (12 pence = 1 shilling) for a quart of beer or cider, though cider was half that price when bought from a farmer. A side of venison ran 9 pence and would feed a large family for a week. Fish was also cheap. A 12-pound cod went for two pence.

Shelter was also inexpensive: a cottage could be rented for just a few shillings a month.

Other necessities came high. A lack of tallow resulted in a shortage of candles and a high price for those that could be found. The poor people dipped dried reeds in melted fat, creating a variation of the candle which gave off immense amounts of smoke and almost no light. The less fastidious burned pine needles, putting up with the dripping tar that marred their homes.

Clothing was also costly. The only good aspect of Puritan fashion was that it changed so slowly a woman could wear the same dress for most of her life and never be out of style.

The only thing the Puritan leaders were not able to regulate was the number of coins circulating throughout the colony. The settlers had brought little or no money with them on their long voyage from England. The mother country also passed a law making it illegal for anyone to send coins to the colonies. The English leaders felt that colonial exports should be paid for in English goods. For example, the colonists would load a ship with beaver skins, barrel staves, dried fish, and similarly abundant commodities. These would be sent to England where merchants would value them according to what they expected to receive when putting the items up for sale. Then a return ship would be loaded with an equal value of fabric, window panes, mirrors, pewter dishes, liquor, and similar items desired by the colonists.

Such a barter arrangement seemed ideal to the British but was increasingly unpopular with the colonists. They were becoming self sufficient and producing their own furniture and other products which once had to be imported from abroad. The craftsmen in the new world found that timber was in great abundance and that it was a relatively simple matter for a skilled worker to turn out furniture equal to the British products, but at a lower cost. The people found it much more practical to spend their money for local goods when available. But what could they use for money?

At first money was anything someone else would accept. Hopefully a buyer had a few coins but, if not, he might spend up to 12 bullets (the legal limit), valued at one shilling per bullet. Or perhaps he used the multi-colored beads of sea shells the Indians called wampum. Or, if he was lucky, he had been to one of the islands where it was possible to obtain Spanish gold doubloons (1 doubloon = 35 shillings) or silver dollars (1 Spanish dollar = 4 shillings). These could also be used in trade.

Occasionally merchants managed to obtain British money through their business transactions. British troops stationed in the colony were considered British citizens, and coins were sent to the new world to meet their payroll. As a result, some merchants began selling goods to the Army commissary, demanding and receiving payment in coin.

Such a chaotic financial system proved too much for the Puritan leaders. They were outraged by England's refusal to send them coins or allow them to start their own Mint. They felt they were suffering needless abuses and determined to rectify the matter.

The resolution came with a new law, passed in defiance of the laws of England. The law stated, in part: ". . . enacted by the Authority of this Court; that all persons what soeuer haue liberty to bring Vnto the mint howse at Boston all bulljon plate or Spanish cojne there to be melted, & brought to the allay of sterling Silver by John Hull, master of the sajd mint and his sworne officers, & by him to be cojned into 12d: 6d: & 3d peeces, which shall be for forme & flatt & square on the sides & stamped on the one side with NE on the other side with XIId VId, and IIId according to the valew of peeces which shall bee together with a privy marke which shall be Appointed euery three months by the Gouernor, & known only to him & and the sworne officers of the mint. . . .

"And the mint master for himselfe & officers, for their pajnes and labour in melting Refining and Coyning is allowed by this Courte to take one shilling out of euery twenty shillings which he shall stampe as aforesajd."

John Hull was a Boston silversmith who was chosen to be the first mint master for reasons, it is supposed, other than his artistic ability. His early coins were extremely crude, irregular discs of silver stamped with NE on one side and the Roman numerals XII on the other. The value was based on the weight of silver planchet, something the colonists soon learned could be easily altered. Larcenous individuals clipped or filed the edges of the coins, an act which slightly reduced the weight of the coins without damaging the markings. When several coins had been so altered, the silver residue could be quite valuable.

On October 19, 1652, the coinage act was amended so that new types could be used. Again the artistry was crude but at least the design filled both sides of the coin, making unnoticed clipping impossible.

These coins were the famous "tree" pieces. There were Willow Tree Shillings, Pine Tree Shillings, and Oak Tree Shillings. The tree was enclosed in a double ring with the legend MASATHUSETS IN. The double ring design was also used on the reverse along with the legend NEW ENGLAND, AN. DOM. The date and denomination in numerals appeared in the space within the inner circle. No effort was made to adjust the dating to the times. The same 1652 date appears on every coin struck until 1686. The only variation was in the Oak Tree coinage which bore the date 1662 during its entire lifetime.

The Oak, Pine, and Willow Tree Shillings are of secondary interest compared with the man who made them. He was possibly the earliest "huckster" in the new world. Although he was technically a gold- and silversmith, there were few enterprises in which he did not have a hand. He was also extremely shrewd in his business dealings. The contract to produce the coins for the Massachusetts colony, for example, paid him 15 pence for every 20 shillings he produced. This worked out to the exorbitant fee of 6 percent and his contract ran for 35 years. After several years the General Court tried to cancel the contract by buying him off, but Hull refused. He also refused to reduce the fee and the government was held to the original agreement while Hull became one of the wealthiest men in the colonies.

The Hull family lived in a small house on Great Street in Boston. John had been born in Market Harborough, Leicestershire, England, in December, 1624, but the family emigrated to the Colony when he was ten. The elder Hull, once a blacksmith, had accumulated wealth in real estate but became a farmer in Massachusetts.

John had a great fondness for his house, actually just a large, one floor structure. When he grew into adulthood, he moved the chimney from a corner of the room to a more central location. He added a kitchen, covered a lean-to extension of the roof, and greatly enlarged the building into a two story structure, the upper story of which overhung the first. The latter architectural device was not for protection from Indians as many people have assumed. It was a common design of medieval architects which was brought to the colonies by slightly homesick

The Pine Tree Shilling created by John Hull, Colonial mintmaster.

British immigrants who wanted their houses to reflect a touch of their native country.

Hull lived in the house as an adult, too, sharing it with his father until the elder Hull died in 1666. It was a poor location for a silver- and goldsmith, but as Hull once wrote "my Habitation is greatly disadvantaged for trade; yet because I always desired a quiet life and not too much business, it was alwayes best for mee."

John went to school and aided his father in the fields until his eighteenth birthday when he apprenticed himself to Richard Storer, a goldsmith who was his half brother. The term "goldsmith" was a misnomer. Anyone who worked in precious metals of any sort was known as a goldsmith. However, Hull, like most of the goldsmiths in seventeenth century New England, worked in silver and probably never used any gold at all.

There was an economic depression in Boston when Hull went into business. The bulk of the city people had been earning their living selling goods and services to new immigrants. Most of the people who left England were from wealthy backgrounds but could take only a limited number of possessions with them due to the size of the sailing vessels. On arriving in the colony they bought furniture, clothing, and other items. Unfortunately, their heavy spending was immediate rather than continuous. When immigration slackened off, business also went into a slump. The period of 1641–1642 was so bad that many Bostonians had to return to England where they knew they could get jobs. Others reverted to living off the land and the water or started new businesses in the hope that their luck would change.

The new businesses, such as commercial fishing, the exporting of manufactured goods, brought renewed life to Boston. Traders arrived in town with Spanish "pieces of eight," silver coins which could be melted for their metal content, and were then used by Hull to fashion silver pieces for church and home.

Hull showed as little creativity in his church designs as he did with his coins. His better pieces were modeled after silver chalices and other items that had been brought over from England. He was a skilled craftsman but lacked imagination.

Hull married Judith Quincy when he was 23. Governor Winthrop performed the ceremony. Despite the fact that it was a religious service, another year passed before he decided to join the church.

In 1648 Hull became a corporal in the Massachusetts Militia. The Puritans had revived the medieval custom of universal military training and the community call-to-arms in times of trouble. The men took turns at night watch and held monthly armed company drills. They were also subject to the draft in time of Indian wars.

The military brought forth skills Hull had not realized he possessed. He joined an elite group of soldiers known as the Ancient and Honorable Artillery Company and quickly rose to the group's highest rank—captain. This was the second highest honor a colonist could receive and he proudly drilled his troops, dressed in the captain's uniform of russet coat with white lace collar and scarlet swordsash.

Business prospered for all the goldsmiths and Hull soon found himself with an abundance of capital. He invested in a variety of unrelated business including mortgage lending, money lending, the raising of horses, and the purchase of farms. He had a timber cutting business and owned ships which he filled with foods for sale abroad. These boat loads were exchanged for foreign goods of equal value. The European items were then brought back to the colonies and sold to the public at considerable profit. A letter, torn with age, has brought us some insight into Hull's activities. It was sent to John Alden, captain of one of his sailing vessels, on September 18, 1671. Some of the words are missing and have been filled in by guess. It read:

"Mr. Jno. Alden you one the first faire wind to set saile (in the) Keth frendship and to goe to some part of Virginia make (what speed) you can to put off what you carry for good tobacco and so speed (thence to) Ireland what part you think most likely for A markett If you (should) meed with a Good oppertunyty to sell the Keth in Virginia (I grant you) liberty to make A trip home with youre tobacco or ship them (to England or) otherwise, I know not but it may be as good as the other way (of selling it) in Ireland but iff in Ireland remitt the whole by exchange for England and then Invest it into Good mixt serges and prest serges with some lead and shott unless you meet with any such things in Ireland as you know will be better heer and therefore seeing you may spey many Advantages that I heer cannot foresee I leave it to you from first to last in every thinge to doe with vessels and cargo what ever may conduce in youre best Judgement for my reale benifitt and advantage. leave noe debts behind you whereever you goe, I know you will be careful to see the worship of God every day on the vessel and to the sanctification of the lords day and suppression of all prophaines that the

lord may delight to be with you and his blessing upon you which is the
hearty prayer of your friend and owner

John Hull"

With so many business dealings both in Boston and abroad, Hull was
the logical person to whom the Massachusetts General Court would turn
for a solution to its financial difficulties. By 1652 the problem resulting
from a shortage of coinage had gotten completely out of hand. England
had turned a deaf ear to the colonists' plea for specie and the Puritan
leaders did not feel that the people should have to continue using the
mixture of foreign coins, wampum, bullets, and barter objects mentioned earlier.

The General Court took the first rebellious stand against the King and
ordered the coining of shillings which were to weigh three-quarters of
the sterling standard. They felt that the coins would satisfy the needs of
the people and, being substandard in weight, were not likely to be sent
abroad, a situation which would reduce the number available for circulation.

The colony established a mint house that was 16 feet square and 10
feet high, equipping it with tools and all the necessary items for melting,
refining, and coining silver. John Hull was appointed Master of the mint
and ordered to coin "bullion, plate, or Spanish coine" into shillings,
sixpences, and three-penny bits "flatt and square on the sides and
stamped on the one side with NE and on the other with the figure XII^d
VI^d and III^d." For this work he received six percent of the money coined.

Hull did not have time to run the Mint himself so he went into part-
nership with Robert Sanderson, a friend and fellow goldsmith. They
vowed that they would coin all moneys by "the just allay of the English
coine." They followed the law strictly in regards to weight and quality.
When a sampling was assayed by the Royal Mint in 1684, the coins
were found to be of "allay equal to his Majesty's silver Coyns of England" and exactly matching the weight specified by the law.

The cost of coining was outrageous because of Hull's six percent
return. However, every time efforts were made to alter the agreement so
a lesser percentage would be involved, Hull made an annual "donation"
to the colony's treasury. This "donation," actually a bribe, was such a
large factor in keeping the treasury solvent that the issue of his charges
was never debated as strongly as it might otherwise have been.

The Mint proved a boon to business and to the stabilization of coinage. However, it could neither produce all the coins needed for trade nor prevent coins from being shipped out of the country, an action which took place in violation of the law. In addition, most people preferred to export silver bullion and silver coins rather than having them melted and made into Massachusetts shillings. Bullion was accepted abroad at full intrinsic value. Bullion brought to the mint came back in coins worth six percent less than the original bullion as a result of the fee charged by Hull.

After much debate, the General Court decided in 1672 that Spanish dollars could circulate as legal tender. The coins would be rated at six shillings to one Spanish dollar, provided the dollars were first weighed by Hull and then stamped "N.E." These coins continued to circulate even after the Revolution was successful and the colonies were united into a new country. New Englanders were so accustomed to their own shillings that it was many years before they would adopt the official coinage of America.

England was in turmoil when the Massachusetts Bay Colony began issuing its own coins, but following the Restoration, the government took a serious look at what was happening. Sir Thomas Temple was ordered by the Massachusetts General Court to meet with King Charles II to discuss the situation.

Temple decided to pretend naiveté. He lied, telling the King that the colonists had no idea that the coining of money violated the laws of England. They were faced with a serious shortage and knew that the King was so busy with his own problems that he was in no position to order coins for them.

The King asked to examine the coins and Temple handed him one of the oak-tree pieces. He told the King that it was the royal oak and had been placed on the coins as a token of loyalty. The flattery delighted the King, who called the people of Massachusetts "a parcel of honest dogs" and allowed the Mint to continue.

Hull's great wealth was evidenced by his daughter Hannah, an only child on whom her father doted. When she became an adult she fell in love with Samuel Seawall, a man she had first seen at Harvard College. Hull had taken his daughter to the school to see a commencement exercise and Seawall gave his master's oration during the ceremony.

There is an interesting story concerned with Hannah's wedding to Seawall: Hull had his daughter sit on a balance, then matched her weight in Pine Tree Shillings. The exact amount of the dowry is not certain, although one estimate was that it was equal to 30,000 pounds in British money. Other sources claim it was only 500 pounds with 30 pounds paid immediately, 35 pounds a month later and the remainder over a period of time.

Whatever the truth of the matter, Seawall went from rather poor circumstances to instant wealth following his marriage. He was given a large estate to handle and had the money to enable him to pursue both hobbies and politics. He managed the colony's printing press, was a deputy in the General Court, a member of council, a justice of the superior court, and a judge in the infamous special court convened in Salem to hear the cases involving witchcraft. Although he voted for conviction and execution at the time, five years later, after much soul searching, he decided his original beliefs were wrong. He had the courage to publicly admit that he felt he had erred in his judgement at the trial.

When he was 51, John Hull accepted the post of treasurer of the colony. The year was 1676 and King Philip's war was raging. Although the new position was one of great honor, it was to be the most difficult he had ever undertaken.

The financing of the war was handled through successive tax levies passed on the colonial towns. Hull's job was to collect them—a thankless task since 14 such levies were passed in one year alone.

Townspeople often had little money, paying their taxes with barter goods such as fish, corn, and similar products. Hull had to be certain that all the barter goods were of quality, refusing rotting corn and similar items. He then had to sell the commodities for specie which was shipped to England.

Attempting to sell the commodities was difficult. If the people had to use barter to pay the taxes, they certainly could not come up with the money to buy back the barter goods. Hull used his personal line of credit and immense resources to both pay and supply the soldiers. He felt that his money would be returned whenever he was able to sell the commodities. However, when he left the position in 1680, the colony still owed him 1,500 pounds for his efforts.

There was also a second debt to Hull. Shortly after the war began the people of the Massachusetts Bay Colony were offered the chance to buy Maine for 1,250 pounds. Hull raised 700 pounds towards this goal by using his personal bond. The remainder of the money was raised through a loan from London, again using Hull's credit to obtain it.

John Hull died on October 1, 1683 (see Notes). The colonists were indebted to his estate to the sum of 2,125 pounds. In all, he would leave a legacy of less than 6,000 pounds, including the money owed to him. Much of his money had already been lavished on his daughter and son-in-law. However, his personal wealth had been greatly diminished through his years of public service. Hustler though he was, John Hull, Mint Master of the Massachusetts Bay Colony, put patriotism ahead of personal gain.

5

America's Most Abused Coin

Of all the coins produced by the United States Mint, none has been subjected to so much criticism and abuse as the copper Large Cent. The coins, which were struck from the Mint's beginning in 1793 until they were replaced with smaller copper cents in 1857, were both unattractive and poorly designed. Yet, despite their simple appearance, they were to prove far more controversial than any series ever struck in the United States. Even more interesting is the fact that the coins were adapted to assist the public in almost all aspects of their daily life. They would find their way into cooking, medicine, and even the rites of burial.

The Large Cents were originally created to fill a need for a truly American coin which could be readily used for commerce. Prior to the establishment of the Mint, American merchants relied on the coins of England, Spain, and other countries as well as the few circulating Colonial issues in order to conduct business transactions. Unfortunately none of the foreign pieces were useable for very small purchases. The Large Cent filled this void and helped establish a trusted American monetary system that was consistent throughout the country.

Despite the need for the Large Cent, the Congressmen who enacted the legislation to create the coin held the pieces in disdain and refused to make them legal tender. The coins were to serve as little more than trade tokens which merchants would be forced to accept even though they could not be deposited in any bank. The need for small change was so acute that the public at first was enthusiastic about the Large Cent. Only later would it be universally scorned.

The first Large Cent was crude even by the standards of the day. The reverse contained the words UNITED STATES OF AMERI. encircling a chain and the words ONE CENT 1/100. The chain, a device of coin designer Robert Birch, was supposed to be symbolic of the union of the original 13 colonies with the states of Kentucky and Vermont which worked to establish the new nation. There were 15 links, one for each state, formed into the endless chain which he felt symbolized the concept that with unity there was strength and singleness of purpose.

The chain design was not original. James Jarvis had used it in 1787 when he designed the Fugio coppers, produced during the administration of the Continental Congress. It was also seen on the pewter type Continental Dollar of 1776 and on Continental paper money of that same year. It seemed to have had a history which indicated public acceptance of the concept. However, public reaction was quite unexpected.

"Only slaves have chains!" was typical of the comments made when the coin was introduced. "We are not prisoners!" "Our coins should not show the symbols of captivity!"

The March 20, 1793, *Pennsylvania Gazette* ran a letter from someone in Newark which stated, "The American cents do not answer our expectations. The chain on the reverse is but a bad omen for liberty, and liberty herself appears to be in fright. —May she not justly cry out in the words of the Apostle 'Alexander the coppersmith hath done me much harm; the Lord reward him according to his works.' "

So many Americans had migrated from Europe fleeing political oppression that the coins filled them with foreboding. The chain was a bad omen for a new nation.

Slightly more than 36,000 coins had been produced when the Mint Director hastily bowed to public pressure. The chain was removed and a wreath was substituted.

The obverse of the coin was not much better. It was decided that the coins should bear the portrait of Liberty, another symbol for which there was ample precedent.

Liberty's portrait was derived from the concept of Britannia as used on British coins of the 1700's. Like the chain, Liberty was not a new idea for American coinage: she had appeared on the 1776 Massachusetts Pine Tree copper cent patterns and on South Carolina's paper money, among other places. Unfortunately, the American designer managed to free himself from any charges that he might have copied other designs. His rendition of Liberty is totally lacking in artistic merit. The face, featuring what is supposed to be a flowing hair design, looks terrified. Many people felt that Liberty looked mentally defective. She was certainly not the symbol they wanted for the new country.

The chain Large Cent with Liberty "in fright."

A third alteration had to be made that year, this time retaining the wreath concept but introducing a more delicate image of Liberty. She was made to appear dignified and attractive, with her headdress in a style known as the Liberty Cap design.

The use of the Liberty Cap was meant to appease the citizens who had been shocked by the use of the chain on the first coins. Historically, the Liberty Cap dated back to the Phrygians, an ancient people who lived on the Black Sea and managed to conquer most of the eastern section of Asia Minor. The Phrygians, whose civilization was greatest between 1500 and 331 B.C., wore close-fitting cloth or felt caps which both protected them from the cold and, with the narrow brim in front, shielded their eyes from the sun.

The Romans were intrigued by the Phrygian caps and adopted the style, adding the ruling that only free men would wear them. A special red cap of the Phrygian design was given to freed slaves.

The cap was such an important symbol in Rome that when Julius Caesar was killed, the conspirators paraded about the streets with a Phrygian Cap suspended on a spear to represent the fact that the city was free from tyrannical rule. The coins of Cassius and Brutus, two of the murderers, bore the cap between two daggers.

In the 1760's, Britain's John Wilkes used the Liberty Cap when he led the liberal revolt against King George III. Tokens of the period often show Brittania carrying the Liberty Cap on her spear.

The Liberty Cap had also appeared in colonial America. It had been used on the paper money in Georgia and even on the masthead of the newspaper the *Boston Gazette* where it symbolized opposition to those colonists wishing to remain loyal to England.

The early U.S. coinage was rather limited. The Mint was plagued with mechanical failures as well as such problems as an epidemic of yellow fever. The epidemic resulted in the death of Joseph Wright shortly after he had designed the 1793 Wreath Type reverse for the Large Cent. There was also the problem that the American coinage in no way altered the merchants' habit of using foreign coins for business transactions.

The copper used for Large Cents was always hard to come by, and at first, it was felt the coins might be too costly to make. One estimate was that it would cost ten cents for every Large Cent, and this estimate almost convinced Congress to abolish plans for the coin before it had been made. This figure was found to be an exaggeration, although later Large Cents produced between 1851 and 1853 did have a metallic worth greater than their face value.

The result of the high copper price was that the Large Cents became a convenient source of the metal for craftsmen and others who worked with copper. They would buy the cents by the keg, then melt them. This action greatly reduced the number of coins in circulation and was a factor in raising the price of coins selling to present-day collectors to a far higher figure than the coinage records of the Mint might indicate would be fair.

After the initial flurry of interest in the Large Cents, shop keepers became wary of them. It was true that they met a definite need, but the fact that the coins were not legal tender greatly limited their usefulness. Ideally, they could exchange them for silver, but neither the banks nor other merchants accepted them. Many shop keepers got in the habit of tossing the coins into kegs, then selling the kegs for a percentage of the face value of the Large Cents contained inside.

With a great many Large Cents in circulation but few people willing to accept them as money, it became evident that other uses for the coins would have to be found. Among the first people to discover an alternative use were members of the medical profession.

Ringworm had long been one of the minor complaints of the public and the doctors discovered that Large Cents made an excellent treatment for the problem. Patients were instructed to place a Large Cent in a saucer, then to pour in enough vinegar to barely cover the coin. A greenish patina, actually copper sulfate, was formed and this applied to the patient's lesions at frequent intervals. Medical records of the day said it was extremely effective.

An early cure for arthritis was to punch a hole in a Large Cent, put a string through it, then wear one or more coins suspended around the neck. At least one person went so far as to make a belt of Large Cents, probably for the same reason.

Housewives took copper coins into the kitchen. The Large Cents were tossed into kettles of apple butter to prevent scorching during the long hours of outdoor cooking. The women who followed this method would brag that the coins were cleaned at the same time. What it did to the apple butter is not recorded.

Young girls, anticipating marriage and home responsibilities, would ask their mothers for information on the proper way to prepare a variety of foods, including pickles. There was a secret to proper pickle making and once again it involved Large Cents.

"When the barrel of cucumbers has been filled with the brine and vinegar," many a mother told her daughter, "drop in a Large Cent. It will turn those pickles a beautiful shade of green."

What mother did not mention was an important fact she did not know: the chemical action which caused the coin to dissolve and turn the pickles green was actually a poisonous one. If the family was lucky, eating the pickles would only result in a stomach ache they could blame on over-indulgence. If they were not lucky, and many were not, the poison would kill them. Sadly, it was a good many years before the danger of this type of pickle preparation was known.

Undertakers, bothered by the sight of corpses with open, staring eyes, found that the Large Cents made ideal weights for keeping the lids closed. The coins were placed on the eyes and left on the body when it was buried. The practice became so widespread that a common expression, used to describe a particularly reprehensible person, was "He is mean enough to steal the pennies off a dead baby's eyes."

Pharmacists and jewelers filled large glass bottles with Large Cents and placed them in display windows to attract the attention of passers-by. They were also made into tie clasps, cuff links, and ladies' brooches. Some were holed and suspended from necklaces and bracelets.

The coins entered the slave trade, too, a fact which resulted in a coin of relatively high mintage becoming a great rarity. A Salem, Massachusetts, company loaded thousands of Large Cents on a boat sailing to Africa. The coins, which had holes drilled in them, were to be given to tribal chiefs in exchange for slaves who would be brought back to America. On the voyage overseas, a storm came up, sinking the ship and burying a major portion of all the 1799 Large Cents in the ocean. As a result, although almost a million coins had been produced by the Mint that year, today the coin is worth almost as much as the 1793 Liberty Cap issue of which only slightly more than 11,000 were made.

Notched coins were used as a means of identification by those who were fighting slavery in the United States. If a slave was being helped to freedom, he would be given a Large Cent notched in a particular corner —the two o'clock position, for example. White men whose homes were used for hiding the escaped blacks were told where the notch would be for each particular runaway slave. When the slave showed his coin with the notch in the proper location, the white man would give him shelter until he could safely move further north.

Copper is a metal that is easily manipulated and altered, and the large size of the cent made handling easy, despite occasional complaints that the coin was too large for carrying. Many were adapted for mechanical use, some became levers for prying things, others were screwdrivers, a few were notched to serve as gears, and still others were formed into keys.

Holes were cut into many of them, with the shape designed to fit over spindles. They could then turn valve-cocks, tighten clamps, and perform similar services. They were even used as a low-friction base for the central points of gambling wheels.

In New England the Large Cents were considered lucky coins. When a new house, barn, or other farm building was completed, a Large Cent was carefully nailed to the ridge pole. This was said to assure financial success for the family.

When the railroad crossed the new nation, the heavy steam engines proved to be the ideal way for someone to obtain a commemorative souvenir. Trains involved in important events, such as transporting Presidents Lincoln and McKinley to their burial places, were used to flatten coins which had been placed on the tracks. This was so common that the funeral trains often had to slow to a crawl because of the large number of coins placed beneath their wheels.

The reverse of the Large Cent was frequently shaved or ground off so that a message could be added. These souvenir pieces were given away or sold by the organization which prepared them. This first occurred at the 1892 Columbian Exposition, which was held at a time when copper cents had finally become legal tender and when defacing the coins was against the law. However, no one really cared about the Large Cents and the Federal authorities ignored the illegal practice.

A message of a different sort was prepared by people who found that the coins could be altered to shock the person looking closely at them. The "E" in CENT was altered so that the coin would spell an obscenity. Today coins are occasionally owned by collectors who made only a cursory study of their specimens and have not noticed the alterations.

Large Cents have been used as tokens for card games and similar activities. Pitching "pennies" has long been a popular pastime, for example. A similar use for coins was developed by the British who have a pub game called "Shove Ha-penny" which is played with smooth halfpennies on a graduated board. The game is similar to shuffleboard. (Further unusual uses for coins other than the Large Cents will be found in Notes for this chapter.)

Large Cents were used extensively by hotels which wished to mark their room keys. The reverse was shaved off and a room number placed on the back. Then a hole was punched in the coin and it was attached to the key.

Some Large Cents were made into the child's toy "humdinger." Two holes were drilled in the rim, then two loops of cord were passed through them. The cords were wound, then moved back and forth so that the coins would begin to spin very rapidly, producing a humming noise.

Large Cent rims were shaved down and notched by early frontiersmen. The coins were then mounted on rifles to serve as sights.

There are some Large Cents which were regular Mint issues but which appear to have been altered. These are the famous overdates.

The reason for overdating was the desire to avoid waste. The early Mint workers produced dies by hand, a relatively slow process involving so much work that none of the dies were ever wasted. Dies which cracked or were otherwise damaged were kept in use until it was impossible to produce a recognizable coin. If the calendar year changed, rather than throwing away the die, a new date was punched over the old.

Another Mint practice was to prepare coins with dates that omitted the last digit. In that way, only one number needed to be inserted when the die was put into use and the coin would look better than if an overdate had to be produced. However, when the 1799 coinage was complete, there were several unused dies. These had 1800 stamped over them, making an unusual variety. There are even coins with 1800 engraved over 1798, because a few dies were found that had been unused for two years but which were considered too good to throw away.

A few collections of Large Cents are complete with a coin from every year, including 1815 when none were struck by the Mint. In the middle 1800s collectors occasionally altered Large Cents dated 1845 and 1813 to create a coin with the 1815 date. This was done to fill a space in coin holders rather than as an attempt to make illegal profits by passing off the coins as rare issues. To avoid any questions about such activity, many of the collectors altering the coins made it a practice to shave off the reverse and add the words "none made in 1815."

The Large Cents join such select series as the Liberty Head Nickels and the early silver dollars in having an illegally created issue. The coin was the invention of dishonest Mint workers who produced, in 1860, a Large Cent dated 1804.

By the start of the Civil War, coin collecting had become popular enough that there was a premium paid for rare dates. Earlier there had been so little interest that the Mint kept drawers of small change with a trough for coins of each year. Collectors could go and pick out the various coins they sought in whatever condition they desired, paying face value even for rare pieces. The practice ended by the middle of the nineteenth century when the Mint workers became aware of the vast number of collectors who would pay a premium for such coins.

The Mint workers decided to utilize an obverse die for the 1803 Large Cent which they had found all rusted and pitted. Although it was badly deteriorated, they proceeded to re-engrave the die they had discovered, the latter being the reverse for an 1818 Large Cent. The reverse was different from the original 1804 reverse but they were naive enough to feel that no one would notice.

The result is a pitted, ugly coin produced in limited quantity which today commands only a minimum premium in uncirculated condition compared with approximately a thousand dollars for the more numerous, genuine strikes of 1804. It is a coin which is greatly undervalued if the price for other illegal issues is a guide.

It is interesting to note that after the unpopular Large Cent dropped from existence in 1857, it helped spur the business of selling coins in the United States. They were relatively easy to collect so numismatists could get their start in the hobby by taking the coins from circulation. Dealers began to specialize in the coins and went to great lengths to obtain supplies for sale. One commentary on the period was supplied by Ebeneezer Mason, Jr., a coin dealer and writer from Philadelphia. He was a pioneer in the business, following the lead of another Philadelphia man, Edward Cogan, who was the first full time dealer when he opened his shop in 1856. Mason wrote:

"During the years 1857, '58, and '59, the writer was connected with a very popular exhibition, (Apparently an observation balloon taken from town to town and anchored so it floated a few feet in the air—T.S.) traveling from North to South and visiting all the important cities and towns en route. While thus engaged we made it a daily practice to visit all the old junk shops, confectioners, bakers, grocers, etc., and collect all the old and curious coins we could find—at the same time leaving a card with address to establish future trade, and this practice led to a very general hunt in the places aforesaid for coins, and in many instances we were surrounded at the opening of the Exhibition with men and boys eager to dispose of large quantities of old cents, etc. In one instance while passing through North Carolina, we purchased 10,000 copper pieces; 64 brass Washington tokens of 1783, and 46 Connecticut coins, besides a large quantity and variety both foreign and American. These coins or the best of them were disposed of to Mr. Cogan and Mr. Dickeson of this city.

"The gathering of coins afforded us an agreeable pastime, as well as a profitable occupation; and the constant accumulation of coins led us to enter the field as a dealer in this city in 1860. While thus occupied we advertised very extensively in the large cities, offering what appeared to be fabulous prices for rare U.S. cents. Many of our friends will remember the advertisements, headed with glaring capitals: $25 PAID FOR U.S. CENTS OF 1799. (Today worth several thousand dollars—T.S.)

"The public manner in which we made known our wants, induced many persons to send us packages of coins by express and we were obliged to obtain an assistant for the purpose of opening and examining these packages.

"We refer to this matter, as one of the many influences which gave the 'Coin Trade' permanent existence in this country."

Today the Large Cent has found a respected place in American numismatics despite its rather unusual history. Collectors pride themselves on the completion of their sets and some even specialize in the damaged pieces which were used for everything but a medium of exchange. The most unloved coin the nation has ever produced has finally won the hearts of the people.

6

Coins of Australia, New Zealand, and Canada

The coinage stories of the settlers of Australia and Canada are quite different. Australia was a penal colony whose inmates rebelled at the concept of barter for their dealings. Canada's problems were typical of a colony trying to establish a society in a land thousands of miles from the country it was dependent on for almost all supplies. But the settlers did have one experience in common. The money they used was among the most interesting and ingenious ever devised.

Crime control took an odd twist in Britain following the discovery of the new world. Prison did not seem to rehabilitate the dishonest, so why not protect society from the criminal element by removing offenders from the country entirely? Laws were rewritten in the sixteenth century in order to send convicted men and women to British possessions overseas.

When the Massachusetts Bay Colony was established, the British Government thought it was the logical place to send convicts. Many honest citizens were accepting the price of passage overseas from wealthy colonists in Massachusetts. They agreed to work as indentured servants for a set period of time, generally seven years, in exchange for their passage. Would it not be possible, the British officials wondered, to send convicts in a similar manner? The British Government would be paid for the convicts, they would not have to go to the expense of feeding and clothing prison inmates, and the colonists would have an additional source of labor.

The plan worked for a while, but by 1670 the Massachusetts Bay Colony was tired of being the dumping ground for the mother country's

undesirables. They knew the only way they could stop the trade was to refuse to pay for the convict labor. Most of the people ceased the practice immediately although there were enough customers to keep business alive until the Revolution and also when trade was resumed after the war. However, this was minimal when compared with the number of convicts Britain wished to transport.

The practice of transportation of prisoners was an ancient custom going back as far as the Greeks. It was used by Spain, Peru, Denmark, Portugal, France, Sweden, Czarist Russia, and others, although the exact methods varied from country to country. Britain was among the worst in its treatment of prisoners during the trip to the country of exile. The living conditions aboard the prison ships were deplorable and caused the death of many of the inmates. At its best it was as bad as the slave trade, an odd situation since the British detested the idea of slavery. To make matters worse, the crimes for which a person could be exiled were often so minor that a short jail term was considered adequate punishment under revised penal laws a century later. Only those prisoners sentenced to seven years in jail or longer were exiled but such a sentence was possible for stealing food to feed one's starving family.

By 1786 the British government realized that new lands would have to be found for the prisoners. The jails were overflowing and "hulks"— docked ships that were no longer seaworthy—had been converted into places of confinement for the inmates. But even these would not be adequate for long.

On August 18, 1786, Lord Sydney, Secretary of State for Home Affairs in the government of William Pitt the Younger, announced to the Lords Commissioners of the Treasury that the King had decided to use some of the Southwest Pacific territory for the transportation of colonists. It had been 16 years since Captain Cook had begun exploring the Australia and New Zealand areas and the King felt it was time to utilize the land. There was other interest in the land, most notably by the Dutch, so the King was anxious to stake a permanent claim. He saw the transportation of the prisoners to that land as a way to both firmly establish new territory as well as get rid of an undesirable element.

Lord Sydney said, in part "I am, therefore, commanded to signify to your Lordships his Majesty's pleasure that you do forthwith take such measures as may be necessary for providing a proper number of vessels for the conveyance of 750 convicts to Botany Bay, together with such provisions, necessaries, and implements for agriculture as may be necessary for their use after their arrival."

He also outlined a general plan for the area: ". . . for effectually disposing of convicts, and rendering their transportation reciprocally beneficial both to themselves and to the State, by the establishment of a colony in New South Wales, a country which, by the fertility and salubrity of the climate, connected with the remoteness of its situation (from whence it is hardly possible for persons to return without permission), seems peculiarly adapted to answer the views of the Government. . . ."

The new settlement was to be headed by a Governor whose powers would cover both the civil and military aspects of the new land. He would create the positions of justices of the peace, coroners, constables, and other such offices, appointing the men to fill the posts. He would pass judgement on criminals, decide upon fines or other punishment, be able to grant pardons, levy armed forces "for the resisting and withstanding of all enemies and rebels both at sea and on land," and generally maintain firm control of the people. He would have absolute power.

The man selected to be the first Governor was Post Captain Arthur

Phillip, formerly a career Navy man. On what basis the selection was made is not known. Phillip had not had a distinguished career and was living in semi-retirement. Other men had been more highly favored. However, he would prove to be honest, dedicated, incorruptible, and far sighted enough to be able to make long range plans to help the people who would be settling in the new land. For his services he received 1,000 pounds a year in addition to his 500 pounds per year Navy Captain's pay. He had an allowance of 20 pounds per year for stationery and five shillings a day to pay a secretary.

The prisoners were accompanied by a group of Marines who also lived in the settlement, though not permanently. Their commandant would be Major Robert Ross, an unfortunate decision. He had no interest in the success or failure of the convicts in their land of exile. He wanted his marines to tend to their official duties and not make any effort towards helping the prisoners start a new life.

Eleven ships were sent on the initial voyage. All of them of poor quality. One was too small to be safe on such a long journey and another had been rebuilt after a fire burned it to the water line. Most of them handled poorly and none would have been used to transport "important" cargo.

The trip lasted eight months, following a route which took the ships by way of the Canary Islands, Rio de Janeiro, and the Cape of Good Hope. They made regular stops to take on provisions and livestock.

The vessels did not stay together and Phillip deliberately arrived at the island 40 hours ahead of the other ships to make ready for the landing of the prisoners. This separation of the vessels resulted in widely varying treatment of the prisoners. All the Naval officers had been warned against cruelty to the prisoners but only on Phillip's vessel were the orders carried out. On some ships excessive brutality was so common that numerous men and women met their death either from the lash or from untreated injuries and illness. The *Lady Penrhyn*, one of the worst ships, had thumbscrews and leg and wrist irons for the prisoners. Women had their heads shaved and whippings of both sexes were carried out after the prisoners were stripped of clothing. Had the ships sailed close together, Phillip could have checked on how well his orders were being carried out.

Early explorers had described Australia in glowing terms, indicating that survival would be simple and riches would abound. It was felt in England that the convicts would be able to establish a flourishing trade with the mother country, selling a variety of goods. However, a more realistic view was provided by Sir Joseph Banks who saw New South Wales and commented that it had "a soil so barren and at the same time entirely void of the helps derived from cultivation could not be supposed to yield much towards the support of man."

Phillip found that Botany Bay, the scheduled landing point, would not support life. He investigated the area to the north and found there was a perfect natural harbor which he named Port Jackson. By January 26, 1788, the fleet had arrived at the new site. By February 7, the government had been formalized and the community renamed Sydney in honor of Lord Sydney.

The colony's government was supposed to be dominated by the person who was Governor. However, the military remained a strong independent force which often clashed with Phillip's orders. In addition, he received his instructions from the Secretary of State for War and the Colonies, an official who was responsible to the Parliament. However, the distance was such that even major decisions requiring British government approval were made by Phillip, subject to being over-ridden after several weeks when an exchange of messages with the mother country had been made.

The form of government practiced in Australia was technically against British law. However, the area was considered a jail rather than a normal colony and deviations from accepted political practice were allowed. It would only be later, after large numbers of settlers came of their own free will, that changes would occur. As long as the prisoners made up the bulk of the population, autocracy was permitted.

Governor Phillip spent five years in his new position. He quickly learned that his biggest problem would be preventing starvation. The native aborigines had lived off the land for years, but their largely vegetarian diet, supplemented from time to time by eating both the white settlers and each other, was not sufficient to sustain the colonists. Plans had been made for the colony to be self-sufficient within a year but this was to prove impossible. To make matters worse, there were periodic sinkings of supply ships caused by inclement weather and other natural disasters. Scurvy was a problem due to lack of Vitamin C and the convicts often lacked the strength to tend their crops, the result of a diet which often sank below 2,000 calories a day.

Gradually the convicts learned where there was adequate soil which would support growth. They came to understand the widely varying rainfalls and learned to cope with drought. All work was done by hand with hoes instead of plows because there were no horses or other animals capable of pulling a plow. The livestock was minimal, with only 136 animals making up the supply brought over on the boats. As a result the animals had to be bred, not slaughtered for food. Even worse was the fact that the convicts were not given guns so hunting native animals was limited at best.

By the 1800's Australia was considered a home by the people forced to live there. Adequate food was available and social life was becoming normal. Wives and children of the Marines were in evidence and many of the convicts had married women who were exiled to Australia after the initial settlements. There were also settlers who had left England of their own free will to pioneer in the new territory. Goods were in abundance and trade with other countries was becoming a reality.

In 1805, Captain William Bligh was appointed Governor of Australia. Sixteen years earlier he had become famous for surviving a mutiny on his ship, the H.M.S. *Bounty*. He was well known for his heroism and skill both as a seaman and for his success in naval battles against England's enemies.

Bligh took command in August of 1806 and was immediately confronted with a trade problem that was crucial to the colony's success. Farmers with excess produce could not sell it since there was no coinage for its purchase. They could barter for commodities they did not grow but such trades were extremely limiting. They were at the mercy of a system which had no established values. They would frequently make an exchange of goods that was unfair in amounts, the farmers giving up a disproportionately large quantity of produce compared with what they received.

Bligh decided to start a system of barter which was to lay the ground work for an Australian coinage. There were government stores receiving farm products in exchange for other goods, but always on an arbitrary and constantly changing system. Bligh sat down and figured out what commodities the people would need which they did not raise themselves. Then he looked at the type of produce the farmers were bringing to exchange. Finally he drew up a list of fixed rates of exchange, establishing values for all bartered goods so future trades would have to be made at constant rates. He also issued a general order banning "exchange of spirits as payment for grain, animal food, labour, wearing apparel, or any other commodity whatever, to all descriptions of persons in the colony and its dependencies."

Bligh insisted that anyone offering a bill of exchange for payment must state the worth of the bill in sterling. The amount did not matter since coinage was almost non-existent but it was an important starting point. When coins did come into being, values and prices would be known.

Although he made some important changes in the colony's methods of trading, Bligh did not last long in his position. He was arrogant and had a violent temper. He made enemies easily, most of them being part of the group of free settlers who had voluntarily made Australia their home. As a result, pressure was brought to bear and Bligh was forced from the Governorship.

In 1810, Lachlan Macquarie became the new Governor. His appointment followed that of General Miles Nightingall, the successor to Bligh. Nightingall never served in the post since he became ill and had to withdraw from office.

The early years of Macquarie's rule were marked by traditional forms of payment for goods. Without coinage, two commodities had become the standard by which all other items were valued. These were food and liquor. When the new Governor had a huge public hospital built (a building which could handle 300 patients as well as housing the surgeons) the contractors were paid in the form of licenses to import rum.

Macquarie gradually began working for a change in the trading system of the colony. The British government had long held the belief that coinage was unnecessary in Australia; they could not relate to the thought of free enterprise in a penal colony and tried to prevent any British money from being taken there.

The Australians had slowly developed a system of necessity currency and coinage that was rather complex. The government store issued receipts for goods brought in but not traded. These notes qualified the bearer to "buy" a fixed amount of supplies at any time he desired. The notes were readily transferred from individual to individual and were therefore an early form of paper money. There were also personal promissory notes circulating freely, but these were a little more risky. Unless you knew the parties involved in the original transaction, a promissory note might prove to be worthless when accepted for exchange. What few coins trickled into the country from new settlers and seamen from other lands were all rated against the British pound sterling and passed at that valuation.

Macquarie's repeated appeals to the government in London finally brought results. They refused to send British bronze coinage as requested because England was suffering a severe coin shortage due to the heavy expense of financing the war. However, in 1812, 10,000 silver dollars were finally shipped to Sydney.

Silver was highly valued throughout the world and Macquarie was determined to keep the coins in Australia where they were essential. He decided to deface them in such a way that they would no longer be desirable. A machine was made to punch a hole through the middle of each coin. The coin, known as a "holey" dollar, was stamped "New South Wales, 1813," on one side and "Five Shillings" on the other. The piece that had been removed was called a "dump" and was stamped "Fifteen Pence." The combined worth of the holey dollar and the dump was greater than the original value of the dollar.

Later 40,000 Spanish dollars were sent to the colony and the same process was used. The original coin had a value of 4s. 9d. while the two created coins were worth a total of 6s. 3d., giving the government a considerable profit. This concept was not original, however, as it had been used in British colonies facing coin shortages elsewhere in the world, but it is the Australian holey dollar and dump which have survived and they are often seen in museum coin collections.

In 1823, tokens were circulated for coinage. The earliest issue is believed to have been the Tasmanian shilling issued by Degraves and Macintosh, although a flood of tokens would not enter circulation until mid-century. They provided small change and a medium for advertising. There were close to 700 varieties of copper, bronze, and silver tokens circulating throughout the country by the time a British branch mint began operating in Sydney in 1855 following the Australian gold rush.

In 1817, the Bank of New South Wales opened for business and soon added currency to the Australian monetary system. The bank produced a series of notes ranging from two shillings to five pounds, generally marked payable in Spanish dollars.

The Australian gold rush began in 1851 and a branch of the British mint soon followed the influx of men and women seeking their fortune. After more than a half-century of struggle, a permanent Australian coinage was established.

Before leaving the Southern Pacific, it is interesting to note what happened when coinage was introduced to New Zealand. Although this land had been discovered by white explorers even before Australia, attempts at settlement were not made until after the penal colony had been established. The crown then encouraged exploration to increase her territory. This proved successful despite the tendency of the New Zealand native to eat his enemies—a fact which made the whites anxious to make friends.

The New Zealand natives relied solely on barter and often used the exchange method popular with some of the Australian aborigines. This approach involved special meeting grounds where everyone knew bartering was to be handled. One group of natives would go to the trading area, taking the goods they wished to exchange. They would spread them out, then go into the bushes and hide.

The second group of natives would emerge, bringing the goods they wished to trade and placing them near the goods of the first group. Then they would retreat into the brush while the first group returned. If the trade was satisfactory, the first group would gather the barter offering and leave. If it was not, they would leave everything as they found it and go back into the brush. Then the second group would return to add to their offering until a satisfactory agreement could be reached—all without interpersonal contact.

When the first white men discovered them, the Maori, the natives of New Zealand, were living as they probably had during the Stone Age. They had learned to make weapons as well as bone, stone, and wooden ornaments but had not developed the concept of coinage. However, the difficulty they had working with greenstone and its scarcity in their country made articles fashioned from this material extremely desirable. Greenstone ornaments were handled and traded in such a way that they came close to being a form of money.

The initial contact with the natives resulted in barter exchanges. The Maori offered their potatoes and pork for such European trade goods as muskets. Later, as Europeans settled in New Zealand, the Maori became more sophisticated and offered the whites recreation instead of just necessary food supplies. Many Maori men had houses of prostitution for the sailors as well as offering "wives" for naval officers during the duration of their stay. There was also some intermarriage, primarily by sailors who had jumped ship and knew they could not return home without facing a court martial.

The Maori quickly changed from barter to the European system of coinage, but not because they recognized the superiority of that method of trade. The Maori adopted coinage because their customs required them to give valued items to their friends rather than accumulating material possessions. Coins were small and easily concealed. They could be hidden so that no one would know how much wealth a person had. Thus a native could be materialistic without anyone knowing that he was not giving up his wealth to his friends. A description of this situation was given by W. Yates who wrote *An Account of New Zealand* in 1835. He said:

"Barter of every description is now gradually giving way to the introduction of British coin and dollars. One powerful reason why natives preferred money to blankets, clothing, arms, and hardware, was that they were bound in honour to distribute it amoung their friends or, on the first cause of offence, to become dispossessed, but gold and dollars lie in so small a compass, that they can be easily concealed or carried undiscovered about their persons." The only problem was that, "Counterfeit coin has been palmed upon them; medals have been passed for dollars; and even gilded Farthings as Sovereigns." It became necessary for most exchanges to be carried out in the presence of a third party who was capable of vouching for the genuineness of the money.

Turning to colonial Canada and the French, we have another story showing what can happen when people suddenly find themselves without coinage. The year was 1685; the settlement was Quebec. Jacques de Meules was in charge of the settlers in the area known as New France, a colony totally dependent upon the mother country for its coinage.

France always recognized the need for coinage in her colonies and supplied specie to the settlers and soldiers living in New France, unlike England's actions when Australia was settled. The copper and silver pieces were the same that circulated at home and had known value. Unfortunately the number of pieces set aside for the colony was greatly limited. There might have been enough change to handle local needs if the coins were kept in Quebec. Since they were legal tender in France, the colonists used them to pay for imported goods. The merchant seamen took the coins back with them, leaving the people chronically short of change.

At first the colonists tried to make do with barter objects whose values were controlled. Generally this involved the use of either wheat or moose skins, both of which were in demand. Beaver skins might also be used as, to a lesser extent, were wildcat skins and liquor. Each item had a known worth. For example, a blanket always traded for eight cats regardless of where you were in the colony.

Barter was generally considered a coinage supplement and few people liked barter as the exclusive method for doing business. Thus there was a serious problem in the Spring of 1685 when no coinage was to be found in Quebec and the soldiers stationed there to fight the Indians had to be paid. Barter objects could not be used because local merchants refused to accept them exclusively for food and supplies needed by the troops. Money was on its way from France but the journey was long and the need was immediate.

Jacques de Meules was the man to whom the soldiers turned for an answer to their plight. He was in charge of the colony and in a position to take some positive action. Unfortunately, he had no immediate answer and retired to ponder the problem.

What was needed, Meules reasoned, was something that could be used for money until French coins arrived in New France. Whatever was selected had to be available in reasonable quantity and be different from the barter objects normally in use. His answer proved to be a colorful one: he decided to use playing cards.

Playing cards were introduced in Europe as far back as the fourteenth century. King Charles VI mentioned them in his expense account in 1392. By the sixteenth century card decks were similar to the designs we know today. They had 52 cards in four suits and card games were extremely popular.

Soldiers considered playing cards a necessary part of their equipment whenever they traveled. The cards were printed on glossy, high quality paper and could take considerably more abuse than the material used for paper money.

The soldiers' favorite game was called maw, and they played it continuously when they were not on duty.

Meules gathered up all the cards he could find. Some he kept whole. Others he cut into halves and quarters. A full card was valued at four francs. A half card was valued at 40 sols and a quarter card at fifteen sols. Each card was then stamped with the word "bon," signed, and a wax seal applied. Both Meules and a treasury clerk affixed their names to the cards.

The cards were distributed to the soldiers as their pay with the understanding that they would be redeemed for coinage when it arrived from France. The townspeople accepted the card money from soldiers in exchange for goods and services and everyone was happy. Everyone, that is, except the King, who warned Meules that such card money could be dangerous and lead to inflated prices.

Meules decided to drop the playing card money idea after his admonition from the government, but in 1686 another coin shortage forced him to repeat the procedure. As a result, playing card money began to be as widely accepted in New France as official coinage. It was easier to use than barter, and the idea was also adopted by the New England colonies during their periods of coin shortages.

There were several problems with this new approach to money. The first was the ease with which it was counterfeited since almost everyone had access to playing cards. This necessitated severe penalties for counterfeiting. In 1690, for example, a surgeon was condemned to be flogged in the Quebec public square for making card money. When this punishment proved to be an incomplete deterrent, death by hanging became the penalty.

The other problem which arose was the public hoarding of the cards at the early stages when bartering was still a dominant means of exchanging goods. People valued the playing card money and hid it away, thus creating a shortage which had to be alleviated. Meules issued additional card money to cover that which had been withdrawn from circulation but he did not declare hoarded money worthless. As a result, he soon had issued more playing card money than could be backed by the regular shipment of coinage from France. He had created a form of unbacked currency which proved to be as inflationary as the King had feared.

By 1714 there were 2,000,000 pieces of playing card money in circulation. This continued until 1749 when the official issue of paper money for the year had a face value of one million livres.

The use of playing card money gradually decreased and it came to an end in 1760 when the British took control of Canada. But while it circulated it made for one of the more unusual aspects of the history of coinage.

7

California Gold Rush Coins of Necessity

"The whole country from San Francisco to Los Angeles and from the seashore to the base of the Sierra Nevada resounds with the sordid cry of gold! Gold! Gold!!! while the field is left half-planted, the house half-built, and everything neglected but the manufacture of shovels and pick-axes, and the means of transportation to the spot," wrote the editor of the San Francisco *Californian*. The article appeared approximately four months after gold was first discovered at Sutter's Mill, a time when the territory had yet to feel the full impact of the find. The writer of the article would soon abandon journalism in favor of joining the search for the precious metal, which had previously been thought almost non-existent in the United States.

However, the true story of the gold rush and the special coinage which resulted from it begins during a time when few white men had seen California and lived to tell about it.

For many years western expansion had been prevented by the Indians living in the Pacific Coast region. They had a great reverence for the land based on their belief that the earth was the mother of mankind. The idea that any individual could actually own a section of ground was foreign to their way of thinking.

When white men moved West they attempted to secure sections of land for their exclusive use. Soldiers had entered the area, establishing Fort Vancouver in the Oregon territory and other isolated outposts, but the Indians were so numerous and so hostile that conflicts were frequent and no further expansion had been possible. Even the soldiers seldom left the safety of their enclosures.

Indian traders had slightly more freedom since they were not interested in taking any land. But even these men often lost their lives as they moved across the country. There seemed no way to spread "civilization" to this vast unexplored region until the intervention of a force many times deadlier than the gunpowder the white men used in their weapons. That force was disease.

Fort Vancouver provided the first written record of the illness. During July, 1830, many of the soldiers developed chills, a burning sensation, and intermittent fever. The victims were helpless during the course of the disease but the administration of quinine helped most of them pull through.

Medical historians have tried to pinpoint the exact nature of the illness. Some think it was smallpox. Others have suggested typhus, cholera, or measles, none of which seems correct.

Cholera is an ailment that can be spread quickly only if there is a common water supply. Such a supply did not exist for the Indians living along the San Joaquin and Sacramento rivers where the illness reached epidemic proportions. More important is the fact that cholera was well known to the white settlers in the area and they would have been able to positively diagnose it.

Typhus or plague would have had to be spread by rodents such as rats. Because of the vast areas experiencing the disease, a massive invasion of afflicted animals would have been necessary. They would have been most likely to move from the coastal regions eastward, while the disease spread first north and then south.

Measles had plagued the missions during the first few years of the nineteenth century and was well known by explorers. It, too, would have been recognized.

The most likely explanation is that the disease was malaria. It had long devastated the Hawaiian Islands and it would have been easy for mosquitoes infected with the disease to travel with sailors journeying to the Pacific coast. Eventually the disease would so ravage the land that its effects would be felt as late as the 1850's when Sacramento Valley army troops recorded most of their men falling ill. However, by that time it had already done the damage that would allow settlement of California.

It was not long after the disease was first recorded that it began to attack the Indian population. Many of the Indians shook violently, their bodies ached, and their heads filled with pain. They alternated between chills and a burning sensation. Their bodies were so wracked with illness that they were unable to take care of the basic necessities. Many starved to death just a few yards from ample quantities of stored food. They could not move enough to reach it and there was no one left in camp who was healthy enough to care for the sick.

Among the eyewitnesses to the Indians' suffering was Dr. John Townsend, who wrote in his diary: "The Indians of the Columbia were once a numerous and powerful people; the shore of the river, for scores of miles, was lined with their villages . . . The spot where once stood the thickly peopled village . . . is now only indicated by a heap of indistinguishable ruins. The depopulation here has been truly fearful (i.e., near Fort Vancouver). A gentleman told me, that only four years ago (1830), as he wandered near what had formerly been a thickly populated village, he counted no less than sixteen dead, men and women, lying unburied and festering in the sun in front of their habitations. Within the houses all were sick; not one escaped the contagion; upwards of a hundred individuals, men, women and children, were writhing in agony on the floors of the houses, with no one to render them any assistance. Some were in the dying struggle, and clenching with the convulsive grasp of death their disease-worn companions, shrieked and howled in the last sharp agony.

"Probably there does not now exist one, where five years ago, there were a hundred Indians. . . ."

In just four years the densely populated Indian settlements located below the falls of the Columbia River were almost totally destroyed. The river banks were littered with bodies in varying stages of decay. If any members of a community managed to avoid contracting the disease they fled for their lives rather than face the imminent death they felt awaited them in their homes.

Indians living on various islands abandoned their homes and vanished. The Deer Island settlement, 33 miles below Fort Vancouver, was vacated. And the Multnomah Rivers joined together also disappeared completely. Said one visitor to the deserted Wappatoo: ". . . a mortality has carried off to a man its inhabitants and there is nothing to attest that they ever existed except their decaying houses, their graves and their unburied bones, of which there are heaps."

The Cascades region, north of Mount Hood, was apparently the easternmost section of the epidemic. A few survivors were found in the villages and many homes were stripped of possessions, indicating that other survivors may have fled. In some villages witnesses found only half-buried dead.

At the height of the epidemic, one-fourth of all the Indians in the area were dying yearly. The illness would move swiftly through a tribe and there were many stories similar to the one told of the Klackatacks who lived near Fort Vancouver. In 1827, Cassanove, Chief of the Klackatacks, could raise between 400 and 500 warriors from his people. When the illness struck, it took only three weeks to kill every member of the tribe.

The disease worked its way down the coast. It was not until 1833 that California knew the devastation that was being experienced to the north. John Work, a guide who led a party of men from Oregon down the Sacramento River into California, reported seeing large settlements of Indians during the period from August, 1832, to January, 1833. However, after spending some time along the lower San Joaquin, he wrote: "Some sickness prevails among the Indians on the feather river. The villages which were so populous and swarming with inhabitants when we passed that way in Jany or Febry (sic) last now seem almost deserted and have a desolate appearance. The few wretched Indians who remain . . . are lying apparently scarcely able to move. It is not starvation as they have considerable quantities of their winter stock of acorns still remaining. . . ."

Malaria moved swiftly because the Indians lacked the quinine the white men used to successfully treat the disease. What little quinine had found its way into the area belonged to soldiers, settlers, and traders who kept it for themselves.

Another anti-malaria treatment, though one of somewhat questionable value, was the use of a drink made from the boiled bark of the dogwood plant. Many whites claimed to have had their health restored after drinking the liquid.

The Indians knew the health value of dogwood, but they did not use it to fight the malaria. The Indians felt that dogwood was only good for the treatment of horse colic. The medicine was made by boiling the leaves into a strong tea. The horse was then tied to a tree limb, his mouth forced up, and a quart of the tea poured into his nostrils. A drink was also made from the inner bark, but it was used to cure dysentery.

By the time the epidemic was over, the most conservative estimate of the number of Indian dead was placed at 20,000. This means that at least three out of every four Indians living in the Pacific Coast region had succumbed to the ailment. The lack of manpower meant that continued resistance against white migration was meaningless and settlers slowly began drifting into California.

On January 24, 1848, one of these early settlers, James Marshall, picked up a few flakes of yellow metal from the American River where Captain John Sutter had his new sawmill. The metal was gold—a hint of the vast findings to come. It was just nine days before Mexico surrendered California to the United States. News traveled slowly, especially from a sparsely populated area, so neither country's government knew of the discovery at the time the territory was transferred.

When news of the gold finally reached the more populated sections of the nation, the rush for wealth was on. Thousands of Americans made their way West in pursuit of riches. Many would see their dreams fulfilled: in the first five years after the discovery more than 215 million dollars in gold was uncovered. This is in contrast to the 24 million dollars in gold that had been found in all of North America during the previous 55 years.

The westward migration created instant cities in areas that were great distances from the older, established communities to the east. The people were isolated from many of the goods and services they desired. Among the items in extremely short supply were coins, which were essential for businesses to operate.

As history has so often shown, coinage can play a major role in the workings of society, and so it was in California. None of the settlers had bothered to bring much money with them. They carried only the barest necessities when traveling across country, living off the land until they reached California. The bankers, speculators, and financiers who were drawn to San Francisco and surrounding settlements had more foresight but even they were limited in the number of coins they were able to transport. To make matters worse, all the merchandise needed to set up a home was brought by trading ships through the Golden Gate where it was delayed at the Customs House pending payment of import duties. The people had plenty of gold dust and nuggets to meet the payments, but this was not acceptable. According to Section 18 of the Act of August 6, 1846: "All duties, taxes, sales of public lands, debts, and sums of money accruing or becoming due to the United States, and also all sums due for postages or otherwise, to the general post-office department, shall be paid in gold or silver coin only . . . ."

The San Francisco businessmen petitioned the Federal Government for relief from the problems caused by a lack of coinage. They wanted permission to establish gold dust as a fixed medium of exchange or to have the Mint in Philadelphia increase its production of coins so they could obtain an adequate supply. The government proved deaf to the pleas, thus laying the groundwork for private coinage.

The short coin supply and the ready availability of gold dust resulted in immense profiteering among merchants, bar owners, and inn keepers. Gold normally sold for $18 an ounce but the supply was so great that most tradesmen were able to refuse to take it at an exchange rate greater than $12 an ounce, with $8 to $10 an ounce being more common. This meant that the miners were, in effect paying double the Eastern rate for everything they bought from local merchants. Unfortunately they were not in a position to wait the many months necessary to have goods shipped to them so they were forced to pay their bills in gold dust.

Many miners were finding a fortune in gold dust only to discover that their wealth was slipping away due to the inflated prices charged those who did not have coins. Restaurant prices were typical. Better hotels offered meals which began at $2 and soared upwards. It was quite common to pay $1 for "beefsteak, scantily garnished with potatoes, and a cup of good coffee or chocolate . . ." according to one resident.

One restaurant's menu included the following:

SOUPS

Mock Turtle	$0.75
St. Julien	1.00

FISH

Boiled Salmon Trout, Anchovy sauce	1.75

BOILED

Leg Mutton, caper sauce	1.00
Corned Beef, Cabbage	1.00
Ham and Tongues	0.75

ENTREES

Fillet of Beef, mushroom sauce	1.75
Veal Cutlets, breaded	1.00
Mutton Chop	1.00
Lobster Salad	2.00
Sirloin of Venison	1.50

Baked Macaroni 0.75
Beef Tongue, sauce piquante 1.00

The typical diner would spend $5 for a meal, if he was a new arrival who had brought coins with him. A miner might have to use gold dust which would bring double that amount on the eastern market.

Many of the hotel owners and saloon keepers made a fortune selling gold dust back East. They would accept it in trade at one-quarter to one-half of its real value as set by the government, then ship it East and receive full value. They added to their dust supply by sweeping the floors each night, then sifting through the dirt for bits of dust dropped from the carrying pouches of the miners. As much as $200 could be made in this manner each night.

Prices on everything were extremely high. A $10 (New York price) package of drawing paper sold for $164 in California. A $2,000 steam engine brought $15,000. A cheap, dark, tiny basement office cost an attorney $250 a month. Rent at a hotel ran as much as $110,000 yearly.

The idea of private coinage to meet the specie needs of the people had been suggested as early as July 27, 1848. A group of San Francisco citizens suggested that private assayers be allowed to take the gold and shape it into coinlike forms for the payment of customs duties.

When the private coinage was at first refused, the Governor was forced to try and relieve some of the problems through alternate means. He ordered the customs collector to accept gold dust at the standard value of $16 an ounce to meet obligations. This regulation was quickly rescinded by orders of the Federal Government.

Speculators began profiteering. The Governor allowed citizens to deposit gold dust with the customs house at the rate of $10 an ounce. They then had 60 days to exchange legal tender coins for the dust, something they could seldom do. At the end of that period the unredeemed gold was auctioned and the money received used to pay the debts of the miners. The speculators were able to buy the dust for from $6 to $8 with coins which they had been hoarding in anticipation of the sale. This dust could be either spent locally at a small profit or shipped back East for sale at more than 100 percent return.

It was conceivable that foreign coins could be utilized to relieve the problems in California, and many were. Unfortunately their acceptance was based on size rather than intrinsic value. For example, the metal in a French five franc coin was worth seven cents but it was the same size as an American silver dollar. Under the existing regulations the coin was accepted on a par with the dollar at the Custom House. Once again speculators moved in, buying the coins for intrinsic worth and using them at a value equal to their size.

After more than six months the Governor yielded to pressure and established a set value for gold dust. It was officially to circulate at $16 an ounce, two dollars less than the price in the East.

With gold at a fixed rate, it seemed only natural for a private firm to begin striking coins to aid merchants. Norris, Gregg, and Norris produced a $5 coin in Benicia City, California, although the coin was stamped "San Francisco."

The San Francisco brokerage and assay house of Moffat and Company quickly followed and it was to become the most important of all the private California mints. The firm would eventually coin the only private issues to circulate as legal tender.

Soon numerous other firms were issuing coins, most of them in the $2-1/2 to $10 sizes. All the coins were reportedly prepared to the exacting specifications required of the U.S. Mint in Philadelphia when it struck legal tender for the country. For this reason the Federal Government decided that the private mint issues were filling a definite void and permitted the coins to circulate. None of the private minters were prosecuted although the striking of private issues was technically illegal.

In 1851, the harmonious relations the private mints had been enjoying with the Federal Government were shattered. Two U.S. Mint assayers, Jacob Eckfeldt and William DuBois, did an in-depth study of the private mint issues. Their findings rocked California.

Contrary to popular belief, the private coiners were not altruistically attempting to satisfy the public needs with essential specie of genuine value. Instead they were skimping on metallic content so that every dollar was worth only 97 or 98 cents. This does not seem too serious until you consider the large numbers of coins involved.

The only minters whose coins passed inspection were those of the staff of Moffat and Company. Although there were occasional discrepancies between marked weight and intrinsic value, the difference was so slight as to be attributable to nothing worse than human error. One of the worst pieces was a $10 gold coin that was actually worth $9.97.

Despite their good work, Moffat and Company was temporarily put out of business in 1850. Laws were passed establishing the Office of State Assayer; the job went to Frederick Kohler. His duties involved refining and assaying gold dust, then casting it into ingots weighing a minimum of two ounces. These were stamped with the state name, value, and weight in carats. The ingots were legal tender for all debts, a fact which would have been in violation of Federal law except for the fact that California was still a territory and only states had to follow the Federal monetary acts.

During this period private coiners were ordered to redeem everything they had issued at full face value should anyone wish to trade in the coins. Additional provisions made it impossible for them to continue striking gold pieces.

In September, 1850, California became a state. Three weeks later Moffat and Company received a contract to serve as a provisional mint.

In 1851 Moffat and Company struck a new coin, a $50 gold piece which was declared the only legal tender gold coin to come from a private mint. All other private issue coins were refused by banks and most merchants. As a result they were soon melted for their bullion, a fact which has made the once-plentiful California private gold pieces into rare collectors' items today.

On February 21, 1851, a reporter for an Alta, California, newspaper described the new coins. He wrote: "Hexagonal fifty dollar gold pieces, manufactured under an act of Congress, appointing a US Assay office in California, and made under the supervision of the US Assayer, were first issued yesterday. These coins are legal tender, and the coin of the United States Government to all intents and purposes. The coin contains upon one face an eagle in the center, around which are the words, UNITED STATES OF AMERICA. Just over the eagle is stamped 887 THOUS, signifying the fineness of the gold, and at the bottom is stamped 50 DOLLS. The other face is ornamented with a kind of work, technically called 'engine turning,' being a number of radii, extending from a common center, in which is stamped in small figures '50.' Around the edge is stamped the name of THE UNITED STATES ASSAYER."

A $50 gold piece could serve only for extremely large transactions, however. The merchants were still desperate for smaller coins. They petitioned Moffat and Company for lower value pieces at the same time that new private assayers were going to work to solve the coin shortage. Firms such as Wass, Militor & Company and Kellogg & Company began issuing coins worth $10, $20, and even a few $50 specimens. The latter, struck by Kellogg & Co., was a challenge to the supremacy of the official pieces.

Necessity gold coins struck during the time of the California gold rush.

July 3, 1852, marked the beginning of the end for all private mints. Congress passed a law authorizing the establishment of a San Francisco branch mint which would produce all needed coinage for the West.

Construction was slow but by December 14, 1853, work was far enough along so that the United States Assay Office in San Francisco could be closed.

On April 3, 1854, the new branch mint went into operation. Unfortunately, it was undersized and began producing coins more as trial pieces than to meet the needs of the people. In the first nine months it produced $4 million in coins but could only touch upon the needs of the thousands of people living on the west coast. Among other problems, the building office was only 60 feet square, which caused the director to comment to a reporter:

"It is almost impossible to conceive how so much work can be well done, and so much business transacted safely, in so small a space. The entrance to the business office is up a steep pair of stairs and through a dark hall rendered unwholesome by the fumes of acids, and uncomfortable by the noise of machinery and the heat of the engine.

"The apartments of the different officers and the desks of the clerks are cramped and inconvenient, and the vaults depend for their safety chiefly upon the presence of well-tried watchmen." He added that a good lock had been obtained from the Customs House so it could be "placed upon the vault in the treasurer's office, where it was urgently needed."

But the best efforts of the branch mint were not adequate at first. Towards the end of 1854, the private mint of Kellogg & Humbert was created. This firm existed for six years though it stopped striking coins in the latter part of 1855. Although supposedly a much smaller operation, Kellogg & Humbert struck more coins in their years of operation than did the U.S. Mint. Estimates run as high as 50 percent greater, but no matter what the figure, at least one financial observer of the day said that without the private issue coins, most of the businesses in San Francisco would have gone bankrupt for lack of specie.

And so one of the more unusual stories of coinage comes to a close. Privately struck, necessity coins of California have faded into history and with them the drama and excitement of the gold rush which created cities overnight.

8

Dona Josefa–
Heroine of Mexico

The achievements of women in history have always been considered of secondary importance to those of men. There have been numerous women who have made major contributions in science, industry, the arts, and other areas. There have been women who have performed heroic deeds and acts which, if they had been men, would have become the subjects of ballads and legends. Unfortunately, such actions have either been ignored, never recorded due to their "unimportance," or written in such a sketchy fashion that few details remain. Thus when a nation sees fit to honor a woman on its coinage, you can be certain the action she took was one of great heroism and achievement.

In 1942, Mexico honored Josefa Ortiz de Dominguez, the wife of the Spanish Colonial Governor of Mexico at the time of the revolution against Spain. She died in poverty and was almost entirely forgotten by her people, yet her actions were of such importance that she became the first woman ever to appear on Mexican coinage.

Dona Josefa's story really begins on September 16, 1810, in the Mexican village of Dolores. It was Sunday and the people anxiously crowded into the small church where services were being held by Padre Miquel Hidalgo y Costilla.

Padre Hidalgo was a learned man with an intense love for the people. He had studied theology at the College of San Nicolas in Valladolid, where he could have been rector. He preferred to suffer the hardships of being a simple village priest because he thought that this was where he could be most useful. He taught the people how to keep bees, raise silkworms, and grow grapes as well as such crafts as pottery making, wine making, and textile weaving. He hoped that the knowledge would enable the villagers to gain extra income through the products they grew and created.

Under normal conditions the Padre's actions would have been lauded by the government. After all, he was showing subsistence-level people how to improve their circumstances without any expense to the government.

But Mexican life was not normal at that time. The country was split into two groups. There was the so-called aristocracy consisting of the Spanish authorities and the government employees who were almost always of Spanish origin. And there were the native Mexican and Mexicans of Spanish origin who were unconnected with the government, working in the small villages throughout the country. They were the majority but were oppressed by the representatives of a government thousands of miles away.

The seeds of revolt had been forming since the late 1700s, but it was Padre Hidalgo who would foment the first major uprising. He used the church service to ask the people if they were ready to strike against their oppressors. He asked if they were ready to win back the lands that had been taken from their forefathers.

The people responded with a roar of approval. Padre Hidalgo had done so much to improve their lives that they were willing to risk everything for the chance at freedom he was offering them.

The September 16th call to arms had been planned for many months. During that period Padre Hidalgo was in regular attendance at the meetings of a "literary society" in the nearby town of Queretaro. One of its founders was Ignacio Allende, a man more interested in the military than in reading good books. He was the person who had convinced Hidalgo to join.

The meetings were held in the home of Don Miquel Dominguez and his wife Dona Josefa. Don Miquel was the corregidor or governor of Queretaro and, as his position would indicate, he had been loyal to the government in Spain. It was his wife who first began talking of freedom for Mexico and who later convinced her husband to participate in a revolt.

Josefa Maria Ortiz had been born in Mexico City in 1768. Little is known of her early life except for the fact that her parents died when she was young and that she was raised by an older sister. At 21 she entered the college of Vizcainas where she met Miquel Dominguez, a man 12 years older than herself. They were married in 1791. Don Miquel was already governor of Queretaro at the time of the marriage, a position which must have impressed Josefa. She knew he was born a Mexican, a fact which normally would have precluded his ever attaining political success. He would have had to show outstanding abilities far in excess of those normally required of a leader for the Spanish to allow him to take such an important position.

The character traits which helped bring Miquel to power were probably the same ones which led to his being hated by local Spanish and creole aristocrats. For example, he insisted upon following the laws of the Spanish government, including the ones which protected workers in the community's textile workshop. Prior to this the Indians and other peasants who worked in them were locked in at dawn and not released until a set amount of work was done—generally long after dark. This semi-slave labor was cheap, kept costs low, and helped make the owners rich.

The workshop owners appealed Don Miquel's abolition of their abominable practices. The appeal went to the viceroy of New Spain, as Mexico was then known, and eventually to the King. The King not only agreed that the governor was acting properly in enforcing the law but also ordered the owners to pay damages to the workers for the period when they were not obeying the law.

These influences would bring Don Miquel into the revolutionary movement. His wife was a strong influence as well, though to what degree is not known.

There were at least 16 members of the group. Padre Hidalgo, however, was the most vital for he was a man of high status among the people. His words had great influence and he was the only one who could hope to gain enough recruits for the revolutionary army to make it successful.

It is surprising how long the "literary" group went undetected. Perhaps it was because it met in the home of a member of the government that it remained secret for many weeks. Whatever the reason, Hidalgo was able to quietly stockpile weapons and the group made plans to declare independence during the fiesta at San Juan de los Lagos. Large numbers of people would be massed together, making this a time when government troops could be overwhelmed.

Towards the middle of August the authorities realized that the literary meetings were subversive in nature. A secretary for the meetings also worked in the Post Office. Apparently hoping to gain power when the revolt failed, he told his supervisors who passed the information on to the high court in Mexico City. No action was taken at that time, since the Spanish did not take the plot seriously. They held the people in such contempt that they did not believe they were capable of revolt. This was also a period when there were many changes in the hierarchy of Spanish rulers in Mexico. Most of the leaders were not yet organized enough to investigate so "minor" a matter.

By early September the literary group knew that its real purpose had been exposed. Fearful for his life, Captain Joaquin Arias, one of the founders, made a public confession on September 11. A messenger was sent to Mexico City with the information, and by Friday the 14th an order had been relayed that the house of Epigmenio Gonzales was to be searched for the hidden supply of weapons.

Don Miquel was alerted to the fact that he had been named as a protector of the group of conspirators. He knew that he could lessen the bloodshed if he took official action in his role as governor. He ordered the arrest of the men who had been his fellow conspirators, planning to carry out the arrests so slowly that the men would have a chance to escape.

The governor's biggest worry was his wife, Dona Josefa. He knew she was one of the most determined of the conspirators. He realized that she would do anything for liberty for the Mexican people and he feared that she would be hurt if he did not take extraordinary action. He had her locked in her quarters while the arrests of their friends were being carried out.

Dona Josefa was outraged by the planned arrests and fearful of what would happen if the conspirators far from the village were not warned in time. She knew that some could make their escape while others could strike at the government immediately, perhaps succeeding with the revolt they had planned for so long.

Despite her education Dona Josefa was unable to write. She was able to read, though, and fortunately she had access to a newspaper. Slowly she cut words from the pages, arranging them together to form a letter of warning to Captain Allende who was armed for action in San Miguel el Grande in the northwest. When it was completed she signaled to the warden of the jail directly below her room. The warden, Ignacio Perez, was also one of the conspirators and was quite willing to carry the note to Allende.

Dona Josefa Ortiz de Dominguez, Mexican patriot.

When Perez arrived at his destination he learned that Allende had gone to Dolores. The message was given to another conspirator, Juan Aldama, and together they went to find Allende.

On September 16, alerted by Dona Josefa's ingenious message, Padre Hildalgo incited the people to go forth against the Spanish. Men gathered from the country and from their homes around Dolores. They brought whatever weapons they had. Some carried guns, others carried machetes, and still others had simple clubs. They were led by Padre Hidalgo wearing his priestly robes and riding a black horse.

News of the revolt spread quickly and the rag-tag army began to swell in size. Indians grabbed knives and clubs to join the revolt. Creole soldiers, men whose ancestry was Spanish but who were born in Mexico, took their arms and became part of the insurrection. They marched from town to town, defeating the garrisons of soldiers who were caught off guard.

While the revolt was starting elsewhere in Mexico, Dona Josefa decided it was necessary for her to try and save the conspirators who were being arrested by order of her husband. Once again she "wrote" a message with words torn from the newspaper. This one went to Joaquin Arias telling him to free political prisoners and start the rebellion. She did not know that he was a traitor to the cause.

Arias went to the town magistrate with the message. Both Dona Josefa and her husband were charged with conspiracy and arrested. By the time the revolt began under Padre Hidalgo's leadership, Dona Josefa and Don Miquel were under arrest along with 12 others from their literary society. The governor was imprisoned in the Convento de la Cruz and his wife was sent to the Santa Clara convent.

The couple was too popular to be held in the convents for long. Public pressure forced their release, although Dona Josefa was rearrested and quickly taken to Mexico City where the people would not be so sympathetic.

Meanwhile the revolutionary army of Padre Hidalgo and Allende had swelled to an estimated 100,000 as they moved through northern Mexico. Spanish soldiers and government leaders fled in terror. Bishops loyal to Spain told the people their actions were wrong, but to no avail.

When the revolt reached Valladolid, another priest, Jose Maria Morelos, joined the fighting. He had been a pupil of Padre Hidalgo and one of his most devoted followers. He was also of humble birth and was greatly sympathetic to the people.

Hidalgo sent Jose Maria Morelos to the south to form guerrilla fighting teams. During 1811–1812 the guerrillas won victories in mountain battles throughout the territory between Taxco and Acapulco.

With the passage of time the Spanish were able to rally their forces. They had superior arms but they lacked the fighting spirit of the natives seeking to be free. The tide of battle began to turn in favor of the Spanish—at the cost of thousands of lives on both sides.

Unfortunately the rebels lacked the discipline of a regular army and their actions began to resemble those of rioters rather than those of a well-organized fighting force. There was indiscriminate looting and burning of homes. Both peasants and Spanish nobles suffered at the hands of the revolutionaries, a fact deplored by the leaders. Many potential recruits returned to supporting the Spanish because they were in greater terror of what many of the revolutionaries had become.

A price was placed on the head of Padre Hildago and loyal Bishops declared him excommunicated, but the revolutionaries steadily made their way towards Mexico City.

The Spanish leaders were terrified of the approaching army. Masses were said in the Cathedral and the Virgen de los Remedios was carried through the streets. An attack would have met with little resistance since morale was at an all-time low. It was the perfect time for the rebels to move to victory—but they did not.

Despite the urgings of his officers and the readiness of his men, Padre Hidalgo refused to go all the way into the city. He ordered the army to turn back north, stopping the momentum of the revolt and causing many of the men to desert in disgust. Padre Hidalgo went to Guadalajara where he felt his duty was to organize the new government. He assumed that others would conclude the revolt.

Padre Hidalgo issued edicts concerning the administration of a free Mexico. Slavery was to be abolished and the land divided among the Indians. Industries and crafts were to be encouraged and used to elevate the standard of living of the people.

It was only later that the priest rejoined the army, but by then the Spanish were strong enough to defeat him. He and Captain Allende were captured and placed under arrest. Allende was executed and Padre Hidalgo was sent north for trial. Church authorities declared he was no longer a priest; the courts condemned him to death. On July 30, 1811, he was executed and his head cut off. Hidalgo's head, along with that of Allende, was displayed on the wall of Guanajuato for the next ten years to serve as a warning for others contemplating revolution.

Meanwhile Dona Josefa had to endure two more trials. She was imprisoned in the convent of Santa Terese from 1813 through 1817, being released only when she promised not to help the revolutionaries.

The revolution was continued under the leadership of Jose Morelos, the priest Hidalgo had sent south. He secretly trained small armed bands of revolutionaries so he would have numerous, disciplined guerrilla forces, thus avoiding the problem of mob violence which had hurt Hidalgo.

Padre Morelos wrote a constitution for a new Mexican Republic in 1813, before the defeat of the Spanish. He called for equality for all men, an even distribution of wealth, and the elimination of special privileges for the elite classes. He even wanted the wealth of the Church confiscated by the government and used for the benefit of all the people.

Morelos was eventually defeated by Spanish troops under the leadership of Agustin de Iturbide, a wealthy creole who had favored revolt until he learned that his lands would be given to the poor. Morelos was executed without a trial. The revolution was over—at least for that time.

In 1820, Iturbide again switched sides, becoming the self-styled liberator of Mexico. He went to Iguala and produced the Plan of Iguala which was designed to win both the wealthy and the peasants. He rallied enough support to create an independent monarchy, free from the tyranny of Spain. The people were still not free, but they could look closer to home to find the tyrant who was leading them.

Iturbide went to Dona Josefa after he had taken power. He wanted her to be a lady of honor in the court of his wife. The patriot refused; she would not support a self-styled emperor when her life had been spent trying to make her people free to govern themselves.

In 1829 Dona Josefa died a pauper. She had given both her extensive wealth and her life for the people she loved. Yet she was almost forgotten for more than 100 years until, belatedly, her portrait was placed on the 5 Centavo coins which made their appearance in 1942. Variations were made in 1950, 1951, 1954, and 1970, but Dona Josefa was never removed. She remains one of the most beloved women in Mexican history despite the fact that her story was almost totally lost, buried in the reams of material written about such men as Padre Hidalgo.

There are numerous coins honoring other members of the early revolt. Padre Hidalgo appears on 5 and 10 Peso coins, as well as on

Padre Miquel Hidalgo y Costilla, the rebel Mexican priest.

several gold pieces. There is a copper Peso for Padre Morelos, and several other coins relating to that period in Mexican history. However, none are reminders of any greater patriotism or heroism than that of Dona Josefa Ortiz de Dominguez.

9

Confederate Coinage
and Finances

In retrospect it might be said that the coinage and finances of the Confederate States of America were no more chaotic than the government itself. Otherwise intelligent men had split the nation in half without any real idea of what to do with the separate country they had created.

The Civil War seemed a necessary evil to most of the people in the South. They knew that there would be a bloody battle or two and some people would die, but they thought it would all be over in a matter of weeks or, if the Union was persistent, a few months at the most. They reasoned that all they had to do was show the North they were serious about having their own government and the fighting would stop. The nation would be allowed to stay divided.

Such an assumption was, of course, naive. President Lincoln did not want the Civil War but he was determined to do whatever was necessary to re-unite the country, no matter how long it took. Unfortunately the Confederate leaders greatly underestimated their adversary when they met to plan how they would finance their battle against the Government in Washington.

The sad condition of the Confederate treasury was evident from an incident which occurred a few days after it opened its office in a small room in a Montgomery commercial building. There was a used desk, a few chairs, and a rough mat that had been tacked to the floor. The identification plate on the door was just a small card on which someone had scrawled the name of the government department.

The man in charge of the office was Henry Capers, assistant to the Secretary of the Treasury. He was working alone when a Confederate army officer entered the room with an order from President Davis authorizing the Treasury to provide the funds for outfitting one hundred soldiers.

Capers read the order, then reached into his pocket and took out his money. He had approximately ten dollars in currency and change issued by the Federal Government in Washington. "This is all the money there is in the Confederate Treasury at present," he said, sadly.

The Secretary of the Treasury, Christopher Memminger, heard about the incident and immediately went to a local bank, obtaining the money in the form of a loan. Even this loan was not made officially. It had to be a personal loan to Memminger, guaranteed by his own credit. The bank wanted nothing to do with supplying money to so poor a credit risk as the Confederate government. "At the beginning," Memminger later commented about the humble beginnings, "the Confederacy did not have money enough to buy the desk on which the Secretary wrote."

Memminger would later be severely criticized for his handling of Confederate finances, but he was probably one of the best men for the job despite the fact that his appointment was an afterthought. He was born in Germany on January 9, 1803. His father was a soldier serving in the Napoleonic Wars, under the Prince Elector of Württemberg. He was quartermaster for a battalion of foot jägers (sharpshooters) stationed in Heilbronn and met his death a month after his son was born.

Memminger's mother lacked faith in her ability to raise a son by herself. She took the baby and traveled with her parents to the United States, settling in Charleston, South Carolina. The strain of travel and setting up a new life in a strange country overwhelmed her. She died when Christopher was five.

The young Memminger was placed in the care of his grandparents, but they thought he was too much trouble. They left him with a Charleston orphanage and moved to Philadelphia, breaking all ties with the South.

Memminger was a lonely child who buried himself in books as an escape from the unpleasantness of his existence. He was deeply religious, studying theology as well as finance and law. This love carried into adulthood. He was a regular customer of Charleston's used book stores where he would seek obscure volumes of religious philosophy.

Thomas Bennett, a trustee of the orphanage, took a special interest in the young Memminger. He decided to underwrite the child's education and encouraged him to become a lawyer.

Memminger followed his mentor's wishes. He took legal training, specializing in areas relating to finance and commerce. It was a decision which would thrust him into national prominence.

The legal case which made Memminger famous offers an odd contrast to his work as Confederate Secretary of the Treasury. It involved the issue of "sound" money—paper backed with gold and silver—vs. the unlimited issuing of paper.

The case concerned the Bank of South Carolina which had violated state law by refusing to pay gold or silver in exchange for its notes. The bank announced that it would redeem them only for paper money.

The state government was outraged by the situation. It decided to revoke the bank's charter and asked Memminger to represent the government position.

The court battle lasted for months but it was such an important issue that there were extensive daily reports in local newspapers. The news even reached Europe where financial experts were ordered by their employers to take the long sea voyage necessary to be in attendance to hear some of the arguments being presented.

When the case was finally settled, Memminger had won. Unbacked currency remained illegal and the young attorney had distinguished himself as having a brilliant legal mind.

The bank case gave Memminger the reputation he needed to enter national politics but he felt more comfortable working within his community. He became a Charleston alderman and a member of the Board of Education, and he served as a delegate to the State Assembly for 20 years. He also became a trustee for the orphanage where he was raised, devoting much of his energy to improving conditions in the home.

Memminger was never known to be very vocal in the controversy over slavery. He was a liberal on the issue but it wasn't until January, 1860, that he seriously considered the question of secession. Such inaction on so important a matter made his enemies think he was pro-Union. However, he would eventually write the majority report on secession for the South Carolina Convention, a report which was incorporated in the Ordinance of Secession. He later traveled to the Montgomery Convention to help prepare the Confederate States' provisional Constitution.

Despite his prominence, Memminger was actually an afterthought for the appointment as Treasurer. Confederate President Jefferson Davis asked Robert Toombs of Georgia to take the post. Toombs accepted but was later transferred to the Department of State. At the suggestion of

Robert Barnwell, Memminger was appointed Secretary of the Treasury.

There was much bitterness over Memminger's appointment, primarily from politically ambitious Southerners who wanted the job themselves. The British Consul in Charleston, Robert Bunch, reported the mood of the politicians to his government. "Even now it is believed that his (Memminger's) feelings are not enlisted in the movement, the possibility of which he openly ridiculed six months ago," he wrote.

The *Richmond Examiner* called Memminger the most inept member of a cabinet made up of "intellectual pigmies." The editor stated that Davis "added to his own deficiencies (in finance) by an almost inexplicable choice of his Secretary of the Treasury."

Memminger's critics hated the fact that he was born a German. Still others disliked the fact that he was an orphan. And one person commented, "Mr. Memminger's head is as worthless as a pin's head."

In reality, Memminger was probably one of the best men for the post. His actions had made South Carolina's banks the most fiscally sound of all the banks in the South and West. He had a solid record of supporting the issuing of no more paper money than the amount of gold and silver the nation held. His lone flaw, and it would prove a major one, was his total loyalty to President Davis. He would not argue against an unsound money policy if he felt it was what Davis wanted.

Memminger was faced with major problems right from the start. Of prime concern were the lack of funds and the fact that the only source the Southerners had for paper money was a firm in New York. There were neither competent printers nor engravers in the South, nor was there paper for the production of bank notes.

As has always been the case, few Northern businessmen put loyalty over profit. They were quite happy to aid the South as long as the government paid them. The American Bank Note Company of New York, for example, printed treasury notes and bonds for the rebels after the Confederacy was established. However, the shipment was intercepted by the Federal Government and held as "contraband of war."

Fortunately for Memminger, the Confederate headquarters shifted from Montgomery to Richmond. In the new city he was able to find an elderly German lithographer whose skills enabled him to produce bank note paper out of New York and the other items necessary for printing the money from England, at least until the North established an effective naval blockade later in the war.

Paper money was a necessary evil, but Memminger wanted to strike as much coinage as possible. The Confederates seized all Federal mint branches and custom houses within their territory, capturing 6 million dollars in gold and silver. Another 3 million came from loans from several European capitals. Still other gold came from the sale of cotton abroad. The rest of the gold and silver, about 15 million dollars came from a domestic loan floated early in the war when Southerners still felt enough patriotism to make personal sacrifices for the Government.

In addition to the shortage of funds, the citizens of both sides were hoarding all the gold, silver, and copper coins they could find. They feared that paper money would be worthless and they had to protect themselves by keeping only money with an intrinsic value. Small change was rapidly disappearing from circulation and it would only be a matter of months before it would no longer be available for business transactions.

Memminger did not fully grasp the significance of the money problem. He planned only for minor taxes, the establishment of a uniform system of paper money, and the bond issue. The latter plan was one of his better ideas. A loan was offered in May, 1861, to enable the Treasury to obtain all the gold and silver individual Southerners were hoarding.

The public brought gold and silver coins, serving ware, and other precious metal objects to either the Treasury or their local banks which would pass it on. Credit was given for the donations and the government promised to pay back their value in ten years.

The bonds that were offered could only be purchased for specie. They were interest bearing, generally eight percent, with the interest payable in gold.

Memminger had hoped to hoard the precious metals in the Treasury and issue paper money equal in value to the gold and silver being stockpiled. He knew this was the proper way for a government to operate. Unfortunately the Confederacy was so unstable and so new that no one outside the South would accept the paper and even Southerners did so reluctantly. When supplies were bought, ships outfitted, and other goods purchased, payment generally had to be made in coin.

The figures involved in all this are rather frightening. The Confederate government managed to obtain gold and silver worth 25 million dollars. With this money they had to pay for food, clothing, weapons, ships, and countless other items for the several hundred thousand soldiers and thousands of civil servants. To make matters worse, they were fighting an enemy which was spending money at the rate of *3 million dollars a day* to fight the war!

One of the first actions of the Treasury Department was to hire a large number of women clerks at salaries of $500 a year. They were responsible for signing, clipping, and numbering the treasury notes. The action was ordered by the Confederate Congress whose representatives thought that having notes hand-signed would prevent counterfeiting. It was a foolish theory, however. The variations in signatures among the women actually made counterfeiting an easier matter than ever before. No one knew which signatures were valid and which were false.

Memminger, to his credit, thought the employment of the women a needless expense. However, no one ever changed the law, probably because it at least provided employment for women whose husbands were either fighting the war or among its casualties. The work kept them active and, in many cases, saved their families from starvation.

The Congress was growing desperate for coinage. It was decided that any coins would be accepted as legal tender regardless of who made them. One Treasury shipment may be cited as a typical example of the coinage used by the government. It had, among other items, 3 Napoleons, 8 Spanish half dollars, 24 Spanish quarter dollars, 385 U.S half dollars, and 988 U.S. quarter dollars. The coinage was used for making purchases from abroad and paying the interest on bonds.

The Confederates had captured mints at both Dahlonega, Georgia, and New Orleans, Louisiana. On March 9, 1861, the Confederate Congress authorized that the mints be put into operation and that Memminger was to have whatever funds he needed for the work.

The mints' coinage facilities were not in the best of shape. As Memminger studied the situation, he discovered that most of the Federal dies and some of the coinage equipment had been destroyed by mint workers who felt more loyalty to the Federal Government than to the cause of the Confederacy. However, there were enough dies in good shape for the New Orleans Mint to strike 1,240,000 half dollars of the Seated Liberty design. In all, there would be 2,532,633 of the coins struck that year, all identical in design. The Federal Government had already struck 330,000 but there is no way to distinguish them. However, after the initial striking, Memminger concluded that the cost of production was too high to be practical. Despite the desperate coin shortage, he suggested that the mints be closed, at least temporarily.

The idea of closing the mints met with strong opposition. The critics conceded that coinage was expensive, but it was felt that morale would be improved if coins specifically designed for the Confederacy could be introduced. Such an idea had been proposed as early as March 6, 1861, when New Orleans Mint Superintendent William Elmore wrote to Memminger stating:

"When the Government of the Confederate States assumes active control over the operations of this institution, I assume that it will require new dies, with new devices and inscriptions. To procure them will require time. Would it not be well to commence preparations for the new state of things?"

Memminger had expressed some interest at the time. He replied: "I wish you would see some of the persons in New Orleans, who deal in engravings or designings, and procure some designs from them for the various coins and send them here immediately. I would suggest to them to design something new and appropriate to the South, leaving to the North the Eagle and its counterpart."

Elmore knew of only two possible sources for a design. He contacted the National Bank Note Company of New York, a firm that felt war could be good for business if management did not declare itself partisan towards either side. He also contacted the New Orleans architects Esterbrook and Gallier.

The New York firm came up with an interesting design but one which was never used. The description read: "The principal figure, the Goddess of Liberty, seated, holds in her right hand a staff surmounted by the Liberty cap: her left arm rests on a shield, and the left hand on the 'Constitution.' On the shield (there being no coat of arms yet adopted) is shown a portion of the flag of the Confederacy, unfurled; to the left of the figure will be observed sugar cane growing, a bale of cotton, a sugar hogshead, and a bale of tobacco; to the right, cotton in its various stages of growth, as also tobacco.

"On the reverse side is an endless chain composed of fifteen links; South Carolina, having taken the lead, occupies the top link and the other links represent, right and left, and other states in the order of the secess: the remaining blank lines are an invitation to the border states to hasten to inscribe their names within the circle. The stars of the Confederate States are distinct: those of the border states are in the twilight but visible soon, we hope, to stand out as boldly as their neighbors.

"In the center is inscribed the monogram, composed of the letters C.S.A. Twenty dollars has been printed to represent the denomination of the coin. Of course, the design is adaptable to any denomination of our coin."

The mention of the $20 gold piece offers an interesting sidelight. The coin, a "Double Eagle" as it was commonly known, was a major part of large business transactions in both the North and West where it was always in great demand. But the average citizen and most of the businesses never used a coin worth more than $10, and even that sum was a tremendous amount of money. The New York firm was completely out of touch with the needs of the public when it planned its coin design.

Eventually Dr. B. F. Taylor took over the task of designing a Confederate coin. He was Chief Coiner for the mint and would later become secretary and treasurer of the Louisiana Board of Health. He decided to retain the obverse of the Northern half dollars whose dies they already owned, commissioning only a design for the reverse.

The final artwork was fairly simple. There was a shield containing seven stars and topped with a Liberty cap. A wreath of sugar cane and blooming cotton surround the shield. The entire design was encircled with the words "Confederate States of America—Half Dol."

Mass production of Confederate coins never became a reality. The fact that any coins even existed was almost unknown until 1879. As it was, only four of the new coins had been made and they were not produced in the conventional manner.

A. H. M. Peterson, an engraver and die sinker, prepared the coins. He had to use new dies, produced for the coins, since the dies captured from the North had been either destroyed or defaced by the loyal mint workers. The new dies he created did not fit the coinage presses. An alternate means of production was necessary.

Four regular half dollars were used instead of blank dies. The reverses were ground off, then the coins were placed in an old hand-screw press. One coin went to President Jefferson Davis. A second coin went to Dr. E. Ames and a third to Professor Biddle, both of the University of Louisiana. The fourth coin was retained by Dr. Taylor.

Taylor kept both the coin and the die, selling them later. The coin belonging to Jefferson Davis was stolen, an interesting story which he mentioned in a letter to a Philadelphia numismatist named E. Mason Jr. Davis said:

"I had a Confederate coin. It was in my wife's trunk when it was rifled by the Federal officers on board the prison ship on which she was detained at Hampton Roads before and after my confinement in Fortress Monroe. The coins, some medals, and other valuables were stolen at that time. Whether the coin be the same which has been offered to you as a duplicate, I cannot say. It is, however, not true, as published, that it is now in my possession."

The Philadelphia numismatist, Mason, bought the Confederate reverse die from Dr. Taylor, selling it towards the end of the 1870s to J. W. Scott, a New York dealer. Scott also purchased 500 1861 Seated Liberty Half Dollars and shaved seven grains of silver from each reverse. He then restruck the coins using the Confederate die. The coins are readily identifiable because of a flattened obverse and the reduced weight. He had placed the Liberty Seated obverse against a soft piece of brass, then used a hand-screw to make the reverse impression. This reduced the damage restriking would normally cause but slightly altered the face of the coin.

Scott also struck a set of tokens on white metal planchets. The Confederate reverse was used as well as a special obverse which bore the inscription "4 ORIGINALS STRUCK BY ORDER OF C.S.A. IN NEW ORLEANS 1861 ****** REV. SAME AS U.S. (FROM ORIGINAL DIE SCOTT)"

A Confederate cent design was also commissioned and, again, a Northerner was hired to execute it. George H. Lovett of New York City created a coin which had an obverse containing the head of Liberty along with the inscription "CONFEDERATE STATES OF AMERICA." The reverse had a wreath of corn and wheat. A cotton bale was at the base of the wreath and the denomination was in the center. He even went so far as to prepare dies and sample coins, but in April, 1861, he realized his actions might make him open to charges that he was siding with the enemy. He refused to deliver the commissioned designs, hiding them on his property. He later sold them to Philadelphia coin dealers J. C. Randall and Captain John Haseltine. They used the dies to strike 55 copper cents, 12 silver cents, and seven gold cents. They then defaced the dies.

Attempts at coinage ended as the violence of the war increased. Coins were needed but costs were so high that the government decided that time and effort were better put into the production of necessities for war.

Memminger had assumed the country would combine taxes, bonds, and paper money to handle finances but the Confederate Congress decided that unsecured paper money and bonds would be the easiest way to pay debts. State bank notes were borrowed for immediate needs while official paper money was in preparation. This interim effort was less successful than hoped because of the lack of uniformity of the notes.

Paper money was begun in a small way. The first notes, issued in 1861, totalled only a million dollars and were all interest bearing. They were of high denominations (50 dollars minimum) and were more like bonds. They had to be signed before transferral and were acquired because of the interest to be paid.

The first battle of Manassas, fought in July, 1861, showed that the Civil War was not going to be of short duration. Large sums of money would be needed almost immediately, and for many months to come. The Confederate Congress authorized the issuing of $100 million in notes in denominations as low as $5. Another 100 million dollars was issued in the form of bonds paying eight percent interest. It was believed that the inflationary aspect of the paper money would be offset by the bonds. This was still a case of paper being backed by paper, and by 1863 inflation was out of control. To make matters worse, the Treasury was authorized to issue 50 million dollars in new paper money every month.

The lack of provision for coinage had created a situation which was eroding the operations of every business in the South. Similar problems, although to a far lesser extent, were also evident in the North.

Trying to adjust to a society suddenly without coinage proved a nightmare for the public. Newspaper editors could not expand their circulation. They had to reject subscription requests unless they were for such a long term that paper money could be used in payment.

Banks told their depositors that checks had to be made out only in multiples of $5. Many people used postage stamps as change, generally relying on the 20 cent denomination. They could be cut in half to handle transactions as small as a dime.

Merchants issued illegal paper money called shinplasters which were notes promising change in goods available from the business. A bar might provide small change in notes redeemable in liquor of a quantity equal in value to the amount of change due the customer. One grocer offered a two cent note redeemable in persimmons. Eventually states, railroads, and cities began issuing shinplasters and these were subsequently legalized in order to facilitate trade throughout the Confederacy. The city of Richmond, for example, had issued $500,000 worth of these small-change notes by 1863.

Another source of money came from the Union Army members who were Confederate prisoners of war. Their greenbacks and coinage were taken and put into circulation. The Southerners, although supposedly supporting their own government, passed the Northern greenbacks at a rate of one greenback dollar for every two Confederate dollars. This would later rise to a ratio of one to four, a fact that so embarrassed the Confederate Congress that in 1864 the use of greenbacks was outlawed. However, the Confederate government continued to stockpile the Northern paper money to pay for its own debts.

The banks attempted to convince the people that the paper money of the Confederacy had value. In July, 1861, they began promoting the soundness of the currency. The public was skeptical, however, fearing that in the unlikely chance that the South lost the war, all their money would suddenly be worthless. A similar reasoning caused European governments to refuse to accept the money.

But the banks persisted. They argued that Confederate currency was every bit as valuable as real property holdings. They said that if the war was lost, the people would have their possessions taken from them as well. It would be better to accept the currency, help stabilize the Confederate Government, and, perhaps, win the war than to refuse it and lose everything in the end.

Newspapers added their voices to the arguments. The *Richmond Daily Examiner* wrote: "The currency of the Confederacy is its life blood and the man or corporation who would discredit or injure it reduces his patriotism to a question of dollars and cents, and ends with poisoning the public confidence in the success of our armies and the integrity of our cause."

While the battle over the paper money situation was raging, the merchants and the people were continuing their attempts to find devices to take the place of coinage. Many merchants manufactured tokens known as copperheads to take the place of cents. These were outlawed in 1863 but continued in circulation for the duration of the war.

Patriotic medals, struck at the start of the war, became change because their silver content had value. One elaborate piece has an obverse showing a cannon, powder barrels, and cannon balls at the base of what appears to be a palm tree. The slogan "NO SUBMISSION TO THE NORTH" surrounds the design. The reverse shows various plants and has the slogan "THE WEALTH OF THE SOUTH" and "Rice Tobacco Sugar Cotton."

Some of the tokens were crudely struck. One silver planchet has seven randomly stamped stars on it. The name "JEFF DAVIS" is stamped on it as well as the derogatory words "King of the South." The latter comment may have been an addition put on by a disgruntled Southerner who had had enough of the war.

Other medals had designs that were of minimum quality. One has an obverse with two crude soldiers manning a cannon and a Confederate cavalry soldier riding along, his sword upraised, on the reverse.

The most successful of the attempts at substitute coinage was begun in the North but used to some extent by both sides. It occurred when the people began turning to the one Federal product which had long been used for business transactions handled through the mail. This was the postage stamp, not only an item officially sanctioned but also one universally accepted in value.

Many people proposed that stamps be used for change. Horace Greeley wrote an article for the *New York Tribune* on July 9, 1862, advocating stamps as small change. He suggested pasting stamps onto a half sheet of paper, then folding the other half over the stamps to protect them. Two days later a Wall Street firm began selling sheets of stamps pasted onto fine parchment and folded in the manner suggested by Greeley. The total value of the stamps on the sheets varied but was always less than a dollar.

Further support came from the *Chicago Tribune* on the following day and, two days later, the Union Congress agreed to the plan. Postage stamps in amounts less than $5 were to be used as change by merchants and the public.

Postmaster General Montgomery Blair was outraged by the situation. The sudden rush to the Post Offices depleted their supplies of stamps and new ones were still in preparation. Profiteers began selling stamps to merchants at up to 25 percent premium over face value.

The love affair the public had with stamps was short lived. You could not carry them around without their sticking together, ruining their potential use. Since they were made of paper they became worn and dirty very quickly and the public thought they should be allowed to return such stamps to the Post Office and receive new ones in exchange. They wanted to make the switch without paying any additional money for the service.

Some merchants tried to make the best of the bad situation by placing the stamps in envelopes and writing the denomination on the outside. They also added a small advertising message as an extra sales gimmick.

Unfortunately the stamps stuck together inside the holder and wear continued to be a problem.

Congress finally rallied to the problem by authorizing the production of stamps without glue. These were to be printed on large sheets of heavy paper. It seemed the perfect answer until the people found they tended to mutilate stamps when they tried to remove them from the sheets.

John Gault, a Boston man, was the one who developed a solution which was to prove one of the more colorful aspects of the Civil War's coin history. On August 12, 1862, he patented a round metal case for holding postage stamps. A thin, transparent mica cover was placed over the stamp to keep it in the holder.

Gault reasoned that if his encased postage stamp idea could be a money maker, he might as well add an additional profit to his merchandise. He made the case in such a manner that it was possible for a merchant to place an advertising message on the back.

Businessmen were delighted with the encased postage stamps and were quite willing to pay a premium to get them. This was the answer to the small change problem. They would raise their prices to cover the cost of the case and still be assured of increased business. They knew that the main reason most people had stopped buying non-essential items was their inability to obtain change. With Gault's device they would be able to conduct business as usual and the people would happily pay a slightly higher price to cover the cost.

Most of the advertising messages were serious for the day but they seem a little humous today. One mentioned "Ayer's Cathartic Pills." Another advertised "Joseph L. Bates, Fancy Goods, Boston." And a third told of "Brown's Bronchial Troches."

Gault's success also proved to be his downfall. His orders were so numerous that he quickly exhausted his supply of stamps. He went to Post Offices in neighboring large cities, only to find that there was an official move to prevent him from getting more stamps for his cases. The Post Office Department had decided that he was buying too many for his enterprise, greatly reducing their stocks for the normal public needs. After just two months producing the encased postage stamps, Gault had to quit the business. He later said he could have made a million dollars that first year if he had just been allowed to continue buying stamps.

The Post Office ruling was not so vindictive as it might first seem. Stamps, unlike coins, have a very short, useful life. To make matters

Fractional currency meant to alleviate the shortage of coins during the Civil War period.

worse, all stamps issued between 1847 and 1851 sent to the South had been seized by the Confederate Government for its personal postage use. The stock of stamps for those years remaining in the Union were recalled and declared worthless to prevent an easy exchange of communication between the North and the South. This meant that new stamps had to be printed just to cover those withdrawn from sale. The Post Office reasoned that it was against the best interests of the public for one man in the city to have so many stamps for his personal use.

Gault was discouraged but determined to stay in business after his initial defeat. He produced encased postage stamps advertising his firm's location and offered to print a company's advertising message on the back as had been done earlier.

The new cases were an improvement on the old. Many were dipped in a tin solution to give them the appearance of being silvered, although this coating quickly disappeared as the cases circulated. The values of the stamps encased in this manner ranged in value from one to ninety cents. Once again the postal authorities put an end to the operation before Gault could enjoy the success that seemed assured.

Additional encased stamps were produced by an employee of the Scovill Manufacturing Company of Waterbury, Connecticut. The company specialized in buttons, tokens, medals, and similar merchandise. The employee had experimented with the encasing of postage stamps shortly after Gault patented the concept. The Scovill cases were either tinned like Gault's or made of brass. They used both the 1861 postal issues and the valueless 1851. It is believed that the latter were used so the cases could be circulated in the South.

There is a theory that Gault once worked for Scovill Manufacturing and that is where he learned to produce buttons and medals, knowledge which would aid in designing his invention. However, the early records of the company were all destroyed by fire and there is no way of knowing if there was really ever any connection.

Despite the run on stamps, the need for change was so great that the encased stamps did little to alleviate the problem. They circulated in both the North and the South, were well received whenever they were available, but never fulfilled the hope of a satisfactory substitute for coinage.

While everyone worked unsuccessfully to obtain something to use as a substitute for coinage, the difficulties with Confederate paper money were getting worse. The notes were always crude and counterfeiting was

An encased postage stamp of the Civil War period. The stamp is covered with a sliver of mica.

a major problem. The official Treasury notes were produced by printers and engravers who were occasionally untrustworthy. They took advantage of lax security to steal and/or forge signatures on the sheets of bills they produced. One man reportedly was caught only after he had stolen $200,000. The death penalty was ordered for counterfeiting, but counterfeiting was too easy and the chance of getting caught was too slim for anyone to be intimidated by the threat.

The major problem was that so many people were signing the notes. A stamping procedure for the name was proposed to the Confederate Congress. Such a stamp would provide uniformity which would make forgery of the signature much more difficult since slight variations could be detected. Unfortunately the bills continued to be hand signed by a wide variety of people. There was no way to tell a forged signature from an authorized one since the handwriting could not be compared from note to note. Even the crudest of forged signatures could have been just the result of an over-tired employee at work.

Counterfeiting was most widespread in the North. The Union Leaders never gave official sanction to the production of counterfeit Confederate notes but they delighted in the devastation they were causing in the Southern economy. Private entrepreneurs actively engaged in the production of large quantities of notes each time a new design was brought North. The counterfeiting activities were probably in violation of Federal laws but the Union turned a blind eye to the counterfeiters and let them smuggle their wares into the enemy's territory in any way possible.

The Confederate Government was always concerned about counterfeiting but could never acquire sophisticated equipment for the production of paper money. The early notes were printed on one side of the paper only, using black ink. Later blue was added for a second tone and both sides of the paper were utilized.

Every change in the Confederate paper money design was meant to thwart the counterfeiters. Unfortunately the counterfeiters improved their skills as the Government improved its money. Worse was the fact that the lack of industrialization in the South meant a lack of skilled engravers and only primitive printing equipment. Such difficulties made the production of notes inconsistent from one to the next. Any two notes could look radically different, yet both might be genuine.

Originally the Register and the Treasurer took it upon themselves to personally sign every note produced. Unfortunately the number needed soon made such action impossible and the clerks were hired.

There were three major Confederate note counterfeiting centers during the war: New York City, Philadelphia, and Louisville. To make matters all the more frustrating for the South, the paper money produced in these centers was frequently accepted by merchants who rejected the legal issues. The counterfeits were better made than the genuine notes so the merchants assumed that the higher quality paper money was genuine!

The best known producer of Confederate money outside the South was Samuel Upham of Philadelphia. He worked with full Union approval, a fact which was kept so quiet that the full story of his efforts will probably never be known.

Upham's counterfeiting began in March, 1862. Within a little over a year he managed to print 1,064,050 different bills. The denominations ranged from fifty cents to $100. He never kept track of the exact monetary value of all his notes but once estimated that their total face value was around fifteen million dollars.

Upham was not really a crook. He was a businessman who happened to undertake an enterprise that was criminal to one section of the country and patriotic to the other. He owned a small store where he sold, according to his correspondence, "patent medicines, perfumery, stationery, and newspapers, foreign and domestic."

The idea for counterfeiting Confederate notes came after an unusual incident occurred in his city. The publisher of the *Philadelphia Daily Inquirer* managed to obtain a $5 Confederate note which he reproduced in the paper. The note was of such great interest to the people that they bought every issue of the paper, then went searching for more.

If the public would buy up all the newspapers to obtain a copy of the note, Upham reasoned, they might be willing to spend the money to get a good reproduction. He went to the paper and bought an electrotype of the $5 bill. He then printed 5,000 copies on French letter paper. He sold them directly to the public at one cent each or to other merchants at a price of 50 cents a hundred. Being honest in his dealings, the margins of each note bore the legend: "Fac-Simile Confederate notes sold, wholesale and retail, by S. C. Upham, 403 Chestnut Street, Philad."

Upham's store carried out-of-town newspapers as well as the local issues. He happened to glance through a copy of New York's *Illustrated Newspaper* and saw that they had run a facsimile of the $10 Confederate note. The engraving had been made by Frank Leslie who sold

Upham the electrotype plate. Once again copies were produced on the French letter paper.

The Philadelphia businessman expanded his printing efforts. He made what he called "curiosities" and "souvenirs of the rebellion." At least that was his public explanation for the Confederate notes he produced; notes which ranged in value to $100. In all he offered 28 different varieties of notes as well as 15 different postage stamps, all of which were heavily advertised in the major circulation newspapers of the North. He did not bother commenting that the advertising line on the bottom of his bills could be clipped and the entire note then passed as genuine. The people who mattered, the ones who would pass the notes in the South, already knew how to handle that little trick.

The Confederacy was as angered and frightened by Upham's work as it was by the power of the Union Army. Both spelled possible ruin. Congressmen meeting at Richmond damned the businessman, and said he had done more harm than the entire army of General McClellan. President Davis even went so far as to offer a $10,000 reward for anyone who would bring Upham to the Confederate capital—dead or alive!

A news story was written about Upham in the Confederate press and was later reprinted by the *Philadelphia Evening Bulletin*. It proved to be good advertising and increased his paper money sales volume extensively. The item read:

"Detective Goodrich, of the Rebel Treasury Department, has exhibited to the editor of the Richmond Dispatch what he terms 'the last and grossest piece of Yankee scoundrelism, and an infernal means to discredit the currency of the Southern Confederacy.' 'It consists,' says the Dispatch, 'in well executed counterfeits of our five dollar Confederate notes, struck off in Philadelphia, where the news-boys are selling them at five cents apiece. This note is well calculated to deceive, and in nearly every particular is a fac-simile of the original. We caution persons receiving this money to be exceedingly careful, as there is no means of knowing to what extent they have been circulated.'

"The 'Yankee Scoundrel' who has counterfeited these VALUABLE notes is Mr. S.C. Upham, 403 Chestnut Street. He has issued fac-similes of seven kinds of rebel shinplasters and two denominations of their notes. He has also issued exact copies of rebel postage stamps of three kinds, the five and ten cent stamps issued by the Confederate Government, and the five cent stamp got up by J.S. Riddell, the postmaster of

New Orleans, and bearing his name. Mr. Upham sells these fac-similes very cheap, but they certainly bring as much as the originals are worth."

The *Louisville Journal* commented, "SAMUEL C. UPHAM of Philadelphia advertises that he will sell Confederate notes at easy prices. We at first thought that he had taken some of them for a very bad debt, but it appears he has executed fac-similes which he disposes of as mementos. The rates offered by Mr. UPHAM are very moderate, and yet we assure all who are anxious to speculate that his lithographed notes are worth just as much as those issued by Jeff Davis."

Upham did receive a comeuppance of sorts in a rather humorous way. The Confederate notes were so varied that few people outside the Treasury were ever certain which designs were genuine. At least one counterfeiter went so far as to create his own paper money design. It had many of the sayings that were on the genuine Confederate notes as well as a few that weren't. The main design pictured a woman riding a deer, an image which had never been used on official Southern currency.

As chance would have it, someone brought Upham the counterfeit bill. He assumed it was genuine and produced thousands of copies which sold as well and passed as easily as the fakes of actual designs!

Even the Confederate treasury experts were limited in their abilities to detect false currency and lesser Government officials found the task impossible. Both fake and real notes were accepted by tax collectors and others. This meant further devastation for the economy because the counterfeits had to be destroyed when discovered, the Government absorbing the financial loss.

In 1864 the Confederate government was becoming desperate. Arrangements were made for all money to be printed in Europe. The foreign mints were more sophisticated in their production methods and had a better chance of producing notes which would thwart most counterfeiters.

Another reason for having the money printed abroad was the hopeless lack of coinage for paying bills. The Government could demand the loyalty of the people within the South, forcing them to accept the worthless paper money. But when it came to dealings with anyone outside the Confederacy, only money with definite intrinsic value was useful as payment. Gold or silver had to be given in exchange for goods.

As we have seen, the Government had almost no hard cash for buying supplies. However, the Civil War came at what proved to be a reasonably opportune time for the South so far as European trade was concerned. "White gold," the cotton crop which made the South famous, was in great demand. A severe shortage of cotton had struck Britain and France as well as other European countries. Cotton was in abundance in the Confederacy, however, and it was the perfect medium for exchange. Arrangements were made to exchange a supply of "white gold" for the printing of the paper money.

The plates were prepared by S. Straker and Sons of London but they were to prove a needless expense. The Union naval blockade had grown so strong that ships were unable to transport the printing plates back to the Confederacy. The plates, in denominations ranging from $5 to $500, were seized by the Union which used them to print an unknown quantity of bills.

It is an interesting sidelight of the war to note that the battles might have been far different if "white gold" had taken a more active role in barter arrangements with Europe. It is believed that if the Southerners had committed their cotton, worth hundreds of millions of dollars, to the war effort, they could have gotten all the assistance they needed from abroad.

Unfortunately the economics of barter were beyond Memminger's training. He ridiculed the idea and refused to take it seriously. It was only much later he would discover, to his regret, that the "white gold" might have saved the Confederacy. By the time he had readjusted his thinking, however, the Union blockade was too effective for any deals with Europe.

Later, while a prisoner in Fortress Monroe, Confederate President Jefferson Davis would comment on Memminger and the issue of white gold. He was quoted as saying: "South Carolina placed Mr. Memminger in the Treasury, and while he respected the man, the utter failure of Confederate finance was the failure of the cause. Had Mr. Memminger acted favorably on the proposition of depositing cotton in Europe and holding it there for two years as a basis for their currency, their circulating medium might have maintained itself at par to the closing day of the struggle; and that in itself would have ensured victory."

Memminger was extremely upset with the post-war critics. He considered the work he had done the best that could be expected. He reminded the people that the 1860–1861 cotton crop had been harvested and sold before the founding of the Confederacy. To make matters worse, by the time the next crop was ready for harvest, the lack of facilities to print bonds or treasury notes would have prevented him from obtaining the paper money necessary to buy it. He failed to mention the fact that the government could easily have appropriated the crop for the good of the Confederacy. He refused to admit that his shortsightedness had compounded the tragedy of the South.

As the war progressed, other ideas for finances were considered. The tobacco crop, it was suggested, could be utilized as backing for the paper money. But tobacco did not have as wide an acceptance as cotton and would not have been good for overseas trade. Since the public trusted only gold, it would also be meaningless to try and use it within the Confederacy.

Someone else suggested that the Confederacy just admit financial defeat and declare its old system of paper money worthless. The government would refuse to pay all debts and the money in circulation would no longer have value. Then the government would issue new money and start fresh. Fortunately this concept was also dropped.

By 1864 the Confederacy was becoming desperate. An elaborate scheme was developed which basically involved forcing the public to exchange non-interest-bearing notes for bonds which paid four percent. Any notes which were not exchanged would be gradually devalued until they were made worthless. This created a certain amount of panic and mass confusion but did little to relieve the problems. To make the situation worse, despite the official devaluation, the old money continued to circulate at the same rate as the new issues in many parts of the South.

To get a better understanding of how the inflation affected the people, it is only necessary to examine the prices paid for goods in the Confederacy devoid of coinage. A boiled ham sold for eleven dollars, coffee went for four dollars a pound, green tea cost seventeen dollars a pound, six-month-old butter cost two dollars a pound, and brown sugar sold for two dollars and seventy-five cents a pound. At the beginning of the war, a fairly wealthy person could scrape together a meal of two eggs, a quarter pound of bacon and an equal amount of butter, coffee and sugar for which she would pay a total of 16 cents. After just a few months, the price of the same food had risen to $4.90.

By the summer of 1864 the Confederate currency system had collapsed and public hostility forced Memminger to resign. George A. Trenholm, a South Carolina banker and businessman, was his successor. In his parting statement, Memminger commented that the economy's condition was not his fault. He said he had been forced "to administer plans which I neither originated nor approved. You know how anxiously I endeavored to provide means to prevent a Redundant Currency. I have always disliked the supporting of the Government by Treasury Notes. But Congress would give nothing but Notes & Bonds— and when we failed to pay specie for Interest the Bonds lost their availableness."

Trenholm's efforts to stabilize the financial situation were extremely effective but came too late to be of any real value. He fought the issuing of more currency, encouraged the public to buy bonds and urged Congress to pass more taxes. He encouraged whatever cotton exporting could be achieved through the blockade in order to obtain foreign credit. This credit would be sold to the public for their paper currency which would be used to pay soldiers and general debts that had long been ignored.

One odd aspect of the Civil War was the fact that the people of the Confederacy seldom related to the events happening all around them. Although their fate and the fate of everything they owned was completely bound up with the fate of the Government, they seemed to see themselves as something apart.

Trenholm encouraged the people to view themselves as members of a large family, with the Government serving as the father. He helped Congress pass a law that allowed the Treasury to be financed by donations from the public, which was encouraged to turn in money, jewels, gold, silver, and public securities. Trenholm led the way by donating personal holdings worth $200,000. The gesture so moved the people that even though the war was obviously in the final weeks with loss seemingly inevitable, the people flooded the Government with donations. The citizens of Staunton, Virginia, for example, contributed 7,100 pounds of bacon, 130 barrels of flour, and $150,000 in bonds. Similar donations flowed in from all parts of the South but it was too late. The contributions could only make a minor dent in the Government debt, which was estimated to be between $400 and $600 million.

By the end of the war Confederate currency had ceased to be a medium of exchange for the people. Unable to find coins, they relied on the tokens mentioned earlier or the ancient system of barter. A rather interesting example of this latter situation is reflected in the letter a society doctor sent to one of his aristocratic patients in South Carolina. He wrote, in part:

"My Dear Mrs. Allston,

"In view of the enhanced price of everything, the Medical Society of this, as well as many other districts throughout the state, resolved two years ago to double their charges. During the last year the large advance in the price of horses and of grain necessary to sustain them, found the medical men entirely unable to live at the rates agreed upon, and they again met as a society and resolved to regulate their charges according to the price of grain and forage leaving it to each individual to do the best he could in arranging with his patients for the means of living. In Williamsburg the medical charges are five times the old rates. So in Charleston, and most of the other cities. I am exceedingly reluctant to adopt any rates, that, with some, might prove prohibitory. I am too well aware that all classes are suffering severely the privations incident to this cruel war, and that in sickness the distress and affliction is tenfold compared with what we have to endure in ordinary health. After mature deliberation, therefore, I have concluded to continue the old rates of charging for all PAST AND FUTURE services to those who will furnish to me grain for forage AT OLD PRICES. In a large number of cases this proposition has been readily accepted as fair and just, and the easiest way to arrive at a rate of charge satisfactory to all parties. Especially does it seem just and equitable to the agriculturists.

"I am willing to receive corn, rice, peas, potatoes, fodder, pork, mutton, lard, butter, eggs, in fact, any and everything that will enable my family to live and feed my horses. Few are aware of my embarrassment, and I would not allude to them, but in justification of the course I have concluded to adopt I have not made one grain for market since 1861 . . ."

And so the war came to an end. The weeks of fighting had dragged out into years. The half-way economic measures that once seemed adequate brought economic chaos to hundreds of thousands of Southerners. All that remains of the Confederacy is a legacy of coins, tokens, and paper money which is among the most colorful and interesting of any period of American history.

10

The United States Trade Dollar

Of all the coins produced by the United States Mint, only one is seldom mentioned, infrequently collected, and was even unwanted during the period when it circulated as legal tender. The United States Trade Dollar, legally produced from 1873 through 1883 and illegally struck the two following years, is considered the black sheep of American coinage. Yet despite the American attitude, the coin was one of the finest silver dollars ever produced. It was so popular abroad that it was found in circulation in the Orient as late as the 1950's.

The history of the Trade Dollar actually begins with the exploration of Mexico by the Spanish and the subsequent discovery of rich lodes of silver. The metal, so valuable everywhere else, was in such abundance that the natives of the area used it for making tools in the same way that people in other countries worked with copper and other more common ores.

The Spanish were quick to establish a mint to take advantage of the rich silver find. Silver dollars struck by the mint were so intrinsically pure that the bullion value of each coin assayed at higher rate than the face value.

Until 1804 the United States Mint coined silver dollars without charge for anyone bringing silver bullion onto the premises. Profiteers found they could buy the Spanish dollars for face value in Mexico, melt them and then take the bullion to the United States Mint. There they received as many as 5 percent more coins than they had had originally. Thus 100 Spanish dollars might be purchased for 100 United States dollars. The Spanish coins were then melted, taken to the U.S. Mint and made into 105 American silver dollars which would be used to buy more Spanish dollars, endlessly repeating the cycle.

As time passed, the quality of the Spanish coins became almost legendary. So many countries knew about the quality of the dollars that they were adopted as the standard for international commerce. American traders wishing to do business abroad, especially in the Orient, had to use the foreign coins. Chinese and Japanese businessmen were skeptical of any new types of coins including the United States silver dollars. They would carefully assay each dollar until they located a series that had a high intrinsic value which was consistent from specimen to specimen. Then they would standardize on such pieces, refusing to deal in other coins. Only the Spanish and Mexican dollars had passed their tests when it came to coinage from anywhere in the Americas.

By the time the U.S. Civil War was coming to an end, exploration of the American West had begun in earnest. Men hoped to get rich by finding minerals of value they thought might be hidden in the land, and their desires were rewarded. For years little silver had been known in the United States but pioneering miners suddenly uncovered the metal in a quantity that seemed to rival the earlier Spanish finds. The Belcher discovery was made in 1864; then came Chollar-Potosi strikes the following year; and in 1866, word of the Hale E. Norcross Bonanza flashed across the continent. Americans would no longer have to import silver bullion. They found themselves with an abundance of the metal and the need to seek new markets for it.

When the initial joy of discovery began to ebb, the men working the silver mines were faced with the harsh reality that their dreams of immense wealth could be shattered. Silver demand had only slightly exceeded the limited supplies in the past. The new lodes brought forth the metal in greater quantity than anyone desired. To make matters worse, silver dollar production had been declining in the United States for many years. By 1850 all the dollars being minted were either melted by jewelers or used for foreign exchange in the few countries which accepted them. The public seldom wanted to be bothered with carrying the coins.

The mine owners turned to Europe for additional markets for silver but the situation abroad was worse than at home. The price of silver bullion was radically unstable. Most foreign governments planned to abandon the metal as a standard for their currencies.

The first country to drop silver was Germany, which adopted the gold standard shortly after the Franco-Prussian War. Silver was retained only for the production of small change, a greatly limited need. The excess bullion was placed on the world market and sold for whatever prices other nations would pay.

France was the next nation to switch to gold, with the other countries quickly following. Minor coinage would still be silver but this meant a sharp reduction in total silver purchases. Foreign silver dollars were rejected by each government and returned to their country of origin. The United States received so many of its dollars back that production of new coins dropped rapidly. Bullion orders were reduced and, by 1874, the Mint was no longer authorized to produce new silver dollars for domestic use.

The silver strikes that men thought would bring them instant riches instead brought panic to the hearts of those who had placed their financial future in the sales of the newly discovered metal. They had a vast supply and a diminishing demand which would soon be so low that they would take a loss on every order they filled.

The only area where silver remained popular was in the Orient. American merchants had been visiting the area since 1784, although their business activities were a minor part of our international trade.

The Oriental commerce had not previously helped the silver interests because customs die hard. At the time when the many American silver strikes were being made, the Japanese, Indians, and Chinese were only accepting the silver dollars struck by Spain and her branch mints in Mexico and Peru. Those coins had been in use since 1600 and had always been consistent in quality. The merchants saw no reason to bother with any other type of dollar for their transactions.

The obverse of the United States Trade Dollar.

What is more interesting is the little discussed fact that even American merchants preferred the Spanish coins to those produced by the United States Mint. Each Spanish dollar was stamped with its weight, fineness, year of coinage, mint mark, and assayer's initials—all details which seemed to assure consistently high quality. Storekeepers felt safer taking one of the Spanish pieces instead of the dollars produced at their country's own mint.

One reason the Spanish coins had circulated so freely in the United States was that the U.S. Mint's production of silver dollars had not equalled domestic demands for many years. When production was finally adequate for the nation's needs, the Spanish pieces were declared no longer legal tender. Banks refused to accept the coins and the public was to stop using them in business. Unfortunately this did not alter the fact that American merchants engaged in international trade still needed the Spanish coins for dealing with the Far Eastern countries. They were forced to go to Mexico in search of the coins where they paid as much as a 7½-percent premium in gold for the silver dollars they needed. Naturally this expense caused great anger.

The fact that American merchants had to pay a premium for the Mexican coins delighted the silver mine owners for it gave them allies in a new cause. Why couldn't the United States issue a special silver coin for world trade? They felt that if such a coin was consistent in content and had a higher intrinsic value than the Spanish coins, traders might be able to convince the Chinese to accept them. They did not mention the fact that the adoption of such a coin would have the side effect of increasing the orders for bullion from their mines.

By 1869 the nation was reunited and many changes were occurring across the land. Mint operations had become extremely diversified. There was the original Mint in Philadelphia and branches in New Orleans and San Francisco. The activities had widened from the early days and Congress was being faced with major legislation regarding the Mint organization and coinage in general. It was felt that it might be wise to establish a Federal Bureau of the Mint in Washington.

With coinage reform in the air, the silver mine owners rushed lobbyists to Washington to bring pressure on the legislators which would result in renewed bullion purchases. They sought to have riders attached to any monetary bills so that the legislation would also have the effect of creating a coin meant for international trade.

A major step towards the change came when Henry Linderman, director of the Philadelphia Mint, resigned his post to work for Congress as part of a committee studying all Mint operations. He was to examine both domestic operations and the various mints in Europe in order to learn how their system worked. His suggestions would be used in the preparation of legislation and he was to be rewarded with the soon to be created post of Director of the Mint Bureau, the only change everyone was in agreement about making.

During this period the silver interests gained a new voice pleading for the trade dollar. Louis Garnett, formerly a refiner and smelter for the San Francisco Mint, spoke out concerning the need for a new coin and discussed how it should look. He envisioned a disc of silver marked with the weight, fineness, and an official stamp of the United States. It would be, in effect, a trade token of guaranteed silver content rather than a legal tender coin of the United States Mint. This idea was not practical, however, because European banks would only accept coins which were legal tender in the nation of origin. His speech was otherwise well received by the legislators, many of whom were convinced of the necessity of establishing a trade coin, although not the token that had been proposed.

On February 12, 1873, Congress passed the much discussed reform legislation to change the Mint system. Both the Trade Dollar and the new Bureau of the Mint were among the proposals included. The coin, which was actually a rider on the main bill, was meant to be used in both domestic and Oriental business transactions. However, the domestic side of the coin was only tokenism. Purchases involving the Trade Dollar were limited to a maximum of five dollars within the United States. The coin would weigh 420 grains, making it heavier and intrinsically more valuable than the Spanish dollars.

The silver interests were elated by what they assumed to be their good fortune. However, they soon discovered that the new Mint Act would not really be of great value to them. With silver dollars being returned to the United States from Europe, the Mint Act called for a halt to the production of silver dollars meant exclusively for domestic use. They were really not needed for they had never circulated freely in domestic trade. The dollars which were not sent abroad were usually hoarded by the public, thus keeping them from circulation. The Mint Act forbade the purchase of bullion for the production of any more of these domestic coins, a detail that was a serious blow to the men who were hoping for increased silver sales.

The Trade Dollar proved an overwhelming success in the Orient. Merchants and bankers were skeptical about it at first, but when the assay reports confirmed that the new coins were consistently more valuable than the Spanish dollars, they were delighted. Profiteers in the Far East decided they would begin buying Trade Dollars with the Spanish 8 reales coins on a dollar for dollar basis, then melt the Trade Dollars for the extra silver they contained. However, this was stopped by a ruling that the Trade Dollar would circulate according to its intrinsic worth rather than its face value.

The use of the trade dollar was best described by a man named William Wright, a newspaperman who wrote under the pen name of Dan DeQuille. In his book *The Big Bonanza*, he wrote, in part: "The Trade dollar was coined for our trade with China and Japan. It was coined expressly to supersede the Mexican dollar in the countries named. It contains a trifle more silver than the Mexican dollar, and the Chinese were not long in ascertaining this fact. Now the American trade-dollar is in great demand in both China and Japan, and the old Mexican dollar is thrown completely into the shade. The Chinese and Japanese are great lovers of silver, and the American trade-dollar being pure silver, is preferred by them to the coin of any other nation. The end—the final fate—of the trade dollar, however is inglorious. It is sent to India by the Chinese for the purchase of opium. In India, the trade dollars are sent to the Calcutta mint and there made into rupees, stamped with the value on one side and on the other, outlandish heathen characters. Thus the silver of the big bonanza fills the opium pipe of the Chinese mandarin. The amount of American silver sent to India to pay for opium is very great."

He went on to mention that Chinese living in towns along the Pacific Coast would gather trade dollars for their employers in San Francisco. These company heads would then ship them on to China. They accumulated so many of the coins that some writers, visiting from the eastern part of the United States where silver coins had disappeared from circulation, actually believed the coins had been produced simply to pay Chinese laborers working in the area.

The Trade Dollar was firmly entrenched in China by the year 1877. A report from a correspondent for one of the large, Oriental banking corporations stated:

"The United States trade dollar has been well received in China and is eagerly welcomed in these parts of the country when the true value of the coin is known. It is a legal tender at the ports of Foochow and Canton in China, and also at Saigon and Singapore. Although not legally current in this colony, it is anxiously sought after by the Chinese, and in the bazaars it is seldom to be purchased. In proof of the estimation in which the trade dollar is held in the south of China, we need only state that the bulk of the direct exchange business between San Francisco and Hong-Kong (which is very considerable) is done in this coin, the natives preferring it to the Mexican dollar. Late advices from San Francisco report that so great is the demand for trade dollars for shipment to China, that the California Mint is unequal to the task of turning out the coin fast enough to satisfy requirements. This is, in our estimation, evidence powerful enough to convince the most skeptical as to whether the United States trade dollar has been a success or not. It is the best dollar we have ever seen here, and as there can be no doubt as to the standard of purity being maintained, it will become more popular day by day, and, we doubt not, ultimately find its way into North China where the people are more prejudiced against innovations."

The overseas popularity of the Trade Dollar was not enough to insure it a long life span. Although trade with the East had increased greatly in recent years, such trade was still a small factor in the economy of the United States. There was no way the production of Trade Dollars could compensate for the loss of bullion sales to the U.S. Mints for production of domestic coinage. Silver was in such abundance with so little demand that it was rapidly being devalued.

Greed and panic took control of the silver interests. The lower the domestic price of silver, the more silver they felt was needed in circulation. They began to work for repeal of the section of the Mint Act of 1873 which banned production of domestic silver dollars. They wanted coinage resumed with no restrictions as to how much bullion could be turned into specie.

The government was no longer controlled by men who would yield to economically unsound concepts such as the silver interests were proposing, however. In 1875 the legislators even went so far as to pass a law which ended the legal use of the Trade Dollar for domestic transactions. This action marked the first and only time in United States history that a coin produced by the United States Mint was not accepted as legal tender by government institutions such as the banks.

The idea behind the new law was to further reduce the silver bullion purchases which were being made. Unfortunately the ramifications of the plan were not thought out. With more than four million Trade Dollars in circulation in the United States, most of them on the West Coast, the public had no intention of stopping their use. Banks had ceased accepting the coins but merchants quickly found that they had to either accept the coins or lose business. If Trade Dollars were all their customers carried in their pockets, Trade Dollars were the coins they would take in payment for their merchandise. It did not matter that the banks would not accept them on deposit.

Since the merchants could not deposit the Trade Dollars in banks, they did the only logical thing they could do. They perpetuated the problem by paying their staff and suppliers with the coins, creating a vicious, seemingly unbreakable cycle.

When merchants had more coins than they could pass on to their employees, they were forced to turn to profiteers who bought them at a discounted price, then used them at full value when trading with other businessmen. A woman might buy a dress for a Trade Dollar, for example, which the merchant would have to sell for fifty cents in legal tender to a profiteer. The profiteer would then go to another merchant and buy a dollar's worth of goods, using the Trade Dollar for payment. Many businessmen went bankrupt while the few that survived considered themselves lucky if they broke even instead of having a steady stream of losses.

The Government's haste in devaluing the coin created economic chaos. The problem could have been avoided by simply asking the banks to retire the Trade Dollars as they were deposited, but this was not done. The business community was being strangled by the consumers who would not do business with a store which refused to accept the Trade Dollar on a par with legal tender silver coins. They bought goods only when the price was maintained at standard levels and they made their purchases almost exclusively with the worthless coins.

The West Coast businessmen suddenly found that they had as great a stake in the future use of silver as did the men who owned the silver mines. They wanted free silver use so they could melt the Trade Dollars and have the bullion made into legal tender coins.

"Free Silver!" was suddenly the battle cry across the land. Politicians began lining up on one side of the question or the other. Men who had worked for passage of the Mint Act of 1873 suddenly claimed they had been deceived by proponents of the act. They lied about their involvement to try and absolve themselves of their roles in an act which had created so much turmoil. They ignored the fact that the consequences of the bill could not have been foreseen. The issue was too hot in the public's mind for them to not take radical stands in order to insure their own re-election.

The Mint Act of 1873 had been far better planned than many of its opponents would admit. Representative Richard Bland of Missouri, known to his colleagues as "Silver Dick," attacked the act as having been hastily produced, although it went through eleven revisions during the three years prior to its passage. He knew that it had undergone intense scrutiny but like his colleagues, he did not wish to have to take credit for such a fiasco.

The silver interests began pouring money into the campaign coffers of men like Bland who would endorse their interests. Congressmen supporting the free silver movement began ignoring the past. One such Representative, Pennsylvania's William Kelley, refused to admit that when the Mint Act of 1873 was under consideration, he had once said: "It is impossible to retain the double standard. The values of gold and silver continually fluctuate . . . Hence all experience has shown that you must have one standard coin which shall be a full legal tender, and then you may promote your domestic convenience by having a subsidiary coinage of silver which shall circulate in parts of your country as legal tender for a limited amount."

Money talked. The Congressmen were grateful for the contributions of the silver interests and free silver became a reality in 1876. Domestic coinage of the silver dollar would be resumed with no limitations placed on the purchase of bullion. The bill was sent to the Senate which twice voted it down. Unfortunately a compromise bill known as the Bland-Allison Act was finally passed into law. This act allowed for both the unlimited production of silver dollars as well as guaranteeing that they could be exchanged for silver certificates in values of $10 or more.

The new act also authorized the Secretary of the Treasury to purchase from two to four million dollars in silver bullion every month, at the current market price, for the production of silver dollars. The weight of the coins was fixed so that the silver content was actually worth only 90.2 cents, leaving the government with a 9.8 percent profit on every coin made. This had the effect of devaluing silver, a fact which greatly upset the mine owners.

But the Government was not through taking what amounted to punitive measures against the silver interests. The devalued silver dollars were used to buy more silver bullion. The amount purchased was equal to the face value of the silver dollars, not their intrinsic worth.

There was strong public sentiment against the bill, but not from most Congressmen. It became law on February 28, 1878, after a veto by President Rutherford B. Hayes was overridden.

Despite some of the problems with the measure, it did seem to be a modest victory for the silver interests. They had, after all, restored the production of silver dollars to the nation and forced the government to increase silver purchases. Perhaps they could go on to influence countries in other parts of the world, they reasoned. They decided to send representatives to an international meeting in Paris on August 16, 1878, to convince the nations attending to return to bi-metallism with fixed ratios of value between gold and silver firmly established.

The European delegates were far more sophisticated in the world of finance than the Americans had given them credit for being. They were neither fools nor would they be the pawns that so many United States politicians had become. They said that a nation should use the metallic base for specie that was most practical for the people, with only gold having a fixed, world-wide value. Silver prices were fluctuating too widely for the establishment of a standard gold-silver ratio. Furthermore, a country's silver resources and mint operations could vary widely from those of other countries so that a standard specie backing was really not possible.

Right from the start, the Trade Dollar had only limited acceptance as legal tender in the United States. Merchants in the West were delighted with the coins at first, of course, so long as they could be deposited in the bank at face value. Free silver seemed a great benefit in conducting their business transactions.

In the South, where cities had been in existence longer than in the West, acceptance of the coin was less widespread. Only the newly freed Negroes took a genuine liking to the coins. They looked upon silver as a symbol of independence. They knew that when they owned silver coins they owned something which could always be melted down for its intrinsic value. Owning coins gave them a greater sense of security than did the paper dollars whites preferred for business.

The rest of the nation rejected the use of the coins. They were used officially for customs duties and taxes but merchants and the general public tended to trade them in at banks whenever they received them in change.

Although there were increased silver purchases, the limited use of silver coins gradually drove the prices down, causing more problems for the free silver interests. By 1885, each silver dollar was worth only 82 cents and the downward spiral continued until 1900 when it reached the ridiculously low figure of 48 cents. There were too many dollars in circulation as a result of the Treasury Department purchases required under the new act.

On February 3, 1883, members of the New York Mercantile Exhange took their complaints against the coins to Congress, marking the start of a year of nationwide protests against the coin. They said, in part: "Some persons employing operatives make a practice of buying these coins at a discount and paying them at par value to their operatives, who again pay them to the retailers of goods, and these, again, pay them to us, and we, not being able to deposit them or pay them in large amounts to our creditors, are compelled to sell them to brokers at a discount for legal money. It results that there is a continual loss falling upon us and a corresponding profit reaped by such unscrupulous persons . . ."

In June, the *New York Times* stated, in part, "These nondescript and bastard coins, which are no more a legal-tender than are the Japanese Yen, which, moreover, are worth less than their nominal value, still circulate in considerable quantities. The Post Office, of course, does not take them; they are refused on railways running out of town, on the elevated roads, but they still maintain their hold in the retail trade. As they are coined purely on private account, every one of them now in circulation has yielded a fraudulent profit to some swindler . . ."

Finally, on December 3, 1883, President Chester Arthur, appearing before Congress, lashed out against the Trade Dollars which he felt were the prime cause of the destruction of the nation's economy. He said, "The Trade Dollar was coined for the purpose of traffic in countries where silver passed at its value as ascertained by its weight and fineness. It never had a legal tender quality. Large numbers of these coins entered, however, into the volume of our currency. By common consent their circulation in domestic trade has now ceased, and they have thus become a disturbing element. They should no longer be permitted to embarrass our currency system. I recommend that provision be made for their redemption by the Treasury and Mint as bullion at a small percentage above the currency market price of silver of like fineness."

At last Congress was convinced of its previous mistakes. Bills were introduced into both houses for removal of the Trade Dollars and a special Congressional investigating committee stated that they must stop. Unfortunately, Representative Bland was still working on behalf of the silver interests and managed to rally enough votes to doom the early efforts for repeal.

Bland agreed to the Government's withdrawing the Trade Dollars from circulation but only if the Treasury would continue to buy bullion at the present rate. He did not want the bullion obtained by melting the Trade Dollars to reduce the purchase of fresh bullion from the mine owners who supported him.

On February 19, 1887, an act was passed to fit Bland's specifications. Trade Dollars would be accepted by banks in exchange for standard silver dollars of equal face value. The Trade Dollars would be melted but bullion purchases from the mines would continue unabated. Only the Trade Dollars not turned in to the banks could be used for foreign exchange. In addition, all previous laws concerning the Trade coins were repealed.

By 1890 it seemed that Congress had gone insane on the subject of silver and coinage. The Sherman Silver Purchase Act was passed, forcing the Government to buy almost twice as much silver as had been purchased under the provisions of the Bland-Allison acts. The Treasury notes had to be redeemed either in gold or devalued silver as the Government saw fit, a fact which caused further inflation and yet another area for potential profiteering.

As silver prices plummeted, the Indian Mint in Calcutta closed its doors, thus abruptly ending purchases by what had formerly been the leading user of silver bullion. Gold was the medium for trade in both Europe and most of Asia. Silver was denounced, paper money rejected, and gold hoarded. Banks were unable to keep up with the demand for coins and, within three years hundreds failed. The United States passed into the financial Panic of 1893.

With the Panic of 1893 creating havoc throughout the United States, President Grover Cleveland went to Congress to demand the repeal of the Sherman Act. He wanted to place the United States on a strict gold standard. He used gold stored by the Treasury to bolster the few remaining banks and to supply specie in exchange for currency that was being turned back to the banks.

It had been twenty years since the silver interests brought the Trade

Dollar into existence and the final result was economic disaster for the United States. The nation was hit by a depression from which it would take many years to recover. But for the world, economic transition to the gold standard had at last been accomplished, a change which would stabilize international trade for the first time in almost a generation.

No story of the Trade Dollar would be complete without a mention of the illegal issues of 1884 and 1885, both struck in Proof. Ten coins of the former and five of the latter are known to exist, making them among the rarest of all United States coins.

As has been seen, interest in the Trade Dollar waned in the final years of its striking so fewer and fewer coins were being produced by the Mint. By 1879 only collectors' pieces in Proof were being struck and by 1883 all official coinage had stopped. However, since honesty was not always an honored tradition among Mint Workers, more Trade Dollars would soon be forthcoming.

In 1884 the magazine known as the *Coin Journal* carried advertisements for Proof Trade Dollars, offering them to buyers at $2.50 each. The advertisements had been placed in both the May-June and the September issues by a man named Charles Steigerwalt. Among the Proof coins offered were specimens dated 1884.

There is a strong likelihood that Steigerwalt was innocent of any dishonesty with his promotion and it is equally likely that he did not own any 1884 Proof Trade Dollars. Most likely he placed the advertisement in anticipation of the expected release of the new coins. This is assumed because his advertisements are the only known reference to the 1884 Trade Dollars until 1908. He probably assumed that the Mint would be producing the coins and wanted to generate orders while waiting for the chance to buy them for his stock.

In 1908 news was released of a collection of 15 Trade Dollars bearing the dates 1884 and 1885. Captain John W. Haseltine announced the find, mentioning that the hoard included ten from the first year and five from the second. Interest in the pieces was great and the coins began a rapid rise in value that continues unabated today.

According to Mint records, the 1884 and 1885 Trade Dollars do not exist. Dies were never made and bullion was never ordered for the striking of any coins.

How the coins came into being is highly speculative. In the cases of the 1804 Silver Dollar and the 1913 Liberty Head Nickel, discussed in another chapter, we can be fairly certain of some of the participants in the illegal strikings. But with the Trade Dollars we can only guess that the source was probably the Chief Coiner.

Only the Chief Coiner was capable of producing specimens as perfect as the ones which legitimately exist, not to mention the fact that he had access to all working dies, their hubs, and the presses. Not even the Superintendent of the Mint could have produced the coins without the Chief Coiner's help. He would have had to have been either the source or one of the sources for the illegal issues.

It is possible, of course, that dies for the 1884 Trade Dollars had been prepared in much the same manner as the dies for the 1913 Liberty Head Nickel. However, there is no way the 1885 dies could legitimately have been made. Once again, greed resulted in the creation of 15 great rarities which, officially, do not exist.

11

Two Illegal Issues
of the Philadelphia Mint

Some of the rarest coins ever produced by the United States Mint technically do not exist! The 1913 Liberty Head Nickel, for example, which was one of the first U.S. coins ever to break the $100,000 sales mark and is considered to be worth more than double that figure on today's market, was never authorized. The dies were illegally used to produce the five known specimens.

The 1804 Silver Dollar was created 30 years after the supposed date of issue. It was produced as the result of private enterprise at the Mint and was never meant to circulate as legal tender. Yet its current worth is approximately a quarter-of-a-million dollars!

The 1804 Dollar, unlike the Liberty Head Nickel (to be discussed later in this chapter), owes its existence to good intentions. More than 19,000 silver dollars were officially struck at the Mint during 1804 but, as was the practice of the day, old dies in good condition were used for the striking. These were all dated 1803 and earlier rather than carrying the current year. No attempt was made to alter the date and no coins *marked* 1804 were struck at that time.

1804 was also to prove the last year that silver dollars were produced for more than 30 years. The government had discovered that the coins were not being used for domestic business transactions as intended. Instead the coins were being shipped abroad for international trade where their acceptance was based on their intrinsic worth. Since the coins were meant for home use only, it was decided to stop producing them for a few years while the public relied on half dollars and smaller change.

By 1832 trade with Asia was increasing. Edmund Roberts was asked to act as special agent for the State Department in negotiating treaties with Japan, Malaya, Borneo, Siam, Burma, Cochin-China, and Muscat. He was given a set of blank passports to fill in according to the countries he decided to visit. His appointment was not submitted for the Senate's approval and only a limited number of people ever knew what he was doing. He would travel on the U.S. Sloop of War, Peacock, using the cover story that he was the captain's clerk.

The reason for all the secrecy was the fact that trade among nations was highly competitive. The President did not want rival countries to know what actions he was taking.

The first hint of what was to come was given in a letter Roberts mailed from Batavia on June 30, 1833. In it he said, in part, "I must not omit to mention that presents are widespread in these countries, and are considered as a mark of respect. They render the donor of more or less consequence according to their magnitude. Both in C. China and Siam, among the first questions asked was 'What presents have you for the King,' considering it as a matter of course that you have not come empty handed."

The first trip Roberts took was doubly successful. He negotiated tentative trade agreements with both the P'hra Klang or prime minister of Siam and with Said Said bin Sultan, the Imaum of Muscat. These treaties were shown to the Senate which ratified them on June 30, 1834.

In September of that year Roberts was preparing to return to Asia. The State Department asked him what fairly inexpensive presents could be prepared for presenting to the rulers.

Roberts replied that most gifts the United States could officially provide would be considered cheap and insulting. He commented: "I am rather at a loss to know what articles will be most acceptable to the Sultan, but I suppose a complete set of new gold and silver and copper coins of the U.S. neatly arranged in a morocco case and then to have an outward covering would be proper to send not only to the Sultan, but to other Asiatics." He also suggested ship models, weapons, and other possible presents though these were not seriously considered.

In November of that year, John Forsyth of the State Department complied with the coinage aspect of Roberts' suggestions. He wrote to Mint Director Dr. Samuel Moore saying:

"The President has directed that a complete set of the coins of the United States be sent to the King of Siam, and another to the Sultan of Muscat. You are requested, therefore, to forward to the Department for that purpose, duplicate specimens of each kind now in use, whether of gold, silver, or copper. As boxes, in which they are to be contained, may be more neatly and appropriately made at Philadelphia, under your direction, than they could be here, you are desired to procure them, if it will not be too much trouble, and have the coins suitably arranged in them before they are sent on. They should be of as small a size as is consistent with the purpose in which they are intended; and should be of wood, covered with plain morocco. The color of one should be yellow, and the other crimson.

"You are authorized to draw upon the Department for the value of the coins, and the expense of the boxes."

Only two coins normally produced by the United States Mint were currently not being minted. One was the silver dollar. The other was the Eagle or $10 gold piece. The latter had also ceased to be struck in 1804 though the reason was because the price of gold had risen to a point where the composition of the $10 coin was worth more than the face value.

There were no old dies available for the Eagle and silver dollar of these denominations and no coins were officially being struck in 1834. The coin sets were completed in April of 1835 when Roberts made a return voyage. All pieces should have been dated 1835 and, in theory, a complete set for that date would not include the dollar and Eagle.

However, in May, 1867, an article in the *Boston Transcript* made reference to the incident in a discussion of the 1804 dollar. The writer, W. Elliot Woodward, commented:

"Some time during the Administration of President Jackson a present was received from the Imaum of Muscat, and our Government, wishing to make a proper return to that magnate, caused, amongst other things, a set of coins to be made for him, and the only dollar dies existing being those of 1804, a few pieces were struck from them, one of which was used as intended, one retained in the mint, and one found its way into a private cabinet.

"It may interest numismatists to know that the one sent to Muscat is no longer to be found. The enthusiasm with which coin collecting is pursued may be illustrated by stating the fact that a gentleman of New York City caused an investigation to be made in the palace of the Imaum in 1865, and learned that the dollar was not there, and had not been for a long time."

What had happened? The Mint Director had decided to strike coins

The "illegal" 1804 Silver Dollar.

dated 1804, the last year when records indicated coins were produced. He was not aware that old dies had been used for the earlier coins so no specimens existed with the 1804 date, though in this regard he was not alone. For years collectors had been trying to find an explanation for why silver dollars dated 1804 could not be found.

Most of the stories created about the "missing" 1804-dated dollars involve the sending of large numbers of the coins overseas for various reasons. One story had them used to pay sailors fighting against Tripoli. Another had them shipped to Hong Kong after Huguenots living in the United States complained because the portrait of Liberty looked like Martha Washington. However, they all had a common bond. Each story ended with the shipment of the dollars being lost at sea.

The new coins were struck in violation of a recent law which stated that all coins must bear the current date when produced. Moore seemed to feel that it was more important to comply with the directive ordering the specimen sets than to worry about legal technicalities. Besides, since there were already 1804 dollars struck (he thought) who would be any the wiser?

Unfortunately one of the coins was struck in Proof, a process the Mint was not capable of handling until it received special equipment in 1817. Furthermore, the designs were different from the 1803 coins and they should not have been.

Additional 1804 coins were produced when two duplicate specimen sets were ordered by the State Department and still others were made later, though exactly when and by whom is not known. In all, eight pieces are known to have been struck from the dies designated Type I.

A second 1804 dollar made its appearance in 1858 after John Eckfeldt, the son of George Eckfeldt who had been the foreman of the Engraving Department, got hold of the obverse dies made for the 1804-dated dollar. He combined them with a current reverse die and struck a few specimens for personal use.

It is important to note that these early years of the Mint were noted for workers producing items for personal gain. Franklin Peale, who acted as Chief Coiner from the 1830's until 1854, ran a highly profitable business producing medals for private buyers. Outside artists supplied the casts needed to make reductions for striking, but Peale used Mint employees and equipment for the actual production of the medals. The work was done during normal business hours with the public footing the bills for the non-Government enterprise.

There were numerous other examples of dishonest Mint employees which will not be discussed here. However, to give you an understanding of how such dishonesty could be concealed for many years, it is only necessary to see who the Mint employees were. A close look reveals that most of the higher-ups were interrelated. I would like to quote the best account of this situation which was written by Eric Newman and Kenneth Bressett in their book *The Fantastic 1804 Dollar*. Their volume is the most complete study of the 1804 dollar currently available. They wrote:

". . . During most of the nineteenth century the Mint was actually overflowing in nepotism. John Jacob Eckfeldt, a machinist and blacksmith, moved from Nuremberg, Bavaria, to Philadelphia before the American Revolution and in 1783 made dies for the Mint of North America project sponsored by Robert Morris . . ." "His son, Adam Eckfeldt (1769–1852), did blacksmith work for the Mint in 1792, became a full time employee in 1795, and was Chief Coiner from 1814 until 1839. His son, Jacob Reese Eckfeldt (1802–1872), co-author of *A Manual of Gold and Silver Coins of All Nations* and its supplements, began at the Mint in the assaying department in 1832 and continued for forty years. The latter's son, Jacob Bausch Eckfeldt (1846–1938) began at the Mint in 1865, worked his way up to Assayer in 1881, and was in Mint service for over sixty-four years. George J. Eckfeldt, nephew of Adam Eckfeldt, was in the employ of the Mint as foreman of the Engraving Department beginning in 1830 and continuing for over thirty years. John M. Eckfeldt, son of George J. Eckfeldt, became the first Chief Coiner of the San Francisco Mint, serving from 1854 until 1862 and returning in 1874 to that Mint in the capacity of Melter and Refiner for a few months. William E. DuBois (1810–1881) began at the Mint in 1833, married Susanna Eckfeldt (sister of Jacob Reese Eckfeldt) in 1840, and eventually became Assayer on the death of his brother-in-law in 1872. The mother of William E. DuBois was Martha Patterson, the daughter of Robert Patterson (Mint Director 1806–1851). Patterson DuBois, the son of William E. DuBois and Susanna Eckfeldt, began at the Mint in 1867 and became Assistant Assayer in 1882. It can be seen that the interrelated Eckfeldt-DuBois-Patterson clan contributed many principal officers in Mint operations for 100 years. James Ross Snowden (Mint Director 1853–1861) was the uncle of A. Loudon Snowden, who began his Mint service in 1857, becoming Coiner in 1866 and Superintendent in 1879. In addition, many other employees were close personal friends of those named."

Is it any wonder that dishonesty, if not condoned, was at least easily kept from becoming public knowledge?

The silver dollars John Eckfeldt produced were taken to local coin dealers and offered for $70 each. The sales were handled quietly but information about them found its way to Director James Snowden. At first he denied that any coins had been struck, but when buyers sent him letters indicating what they had purchased and the price they had paid, he decided to investigate further. He examined the coins and determined that they were genuine Mint products though unauthorized. He confiscated three of the specimens from buyers who had paid $75 each to own them, then destroyed two of them. The third, which was struck over an 1857 Swiss Shooting Thaler, was placed in the Mint Cabinet. It is now part of the collection housed in the Smithsonian Institution in Washington.

Security measures were tightened to prevent a repeat of the incident. Dies not currently in use were to be carefully listed, then locked away. But these measures were in vain. They failed so miserably that when Henry Linderman became Mint Director in May of 1867, he found two sealed boxes of dies not recorded on any of the inventory sheets. One of those dies was for the 1804 silver dollar obverse!

Today only 15 of the 1804 silver dollars are known to exist. Several are in museums, while the ones remaining in private hands are greatly cherished by their owners. Each specimen is valued in excess of $200,-000 yet, technically, they do not exist.

The case of the 1913 Liberty Head Nickel is somewhat different. It might be said that the entire series had a history of dishonesty from start to finish. In Chapter 19 you will read about Josh Tatum gold plating 1883 Liberty Head Nickels, the first year the coins were produced, and passing them as $5 gold pieces. But first we will examine the dishonesty that occurred at the end of this coin's existence.

The Liberty Head Nickel was never a very popular coin during its existence. It was more interesting than the Shield variety which preceded it but artistically the best that could be said about the coin was that it was "functional." The pieces were simple, utilitarian and uninteresting. By 1912 the Mint officials had decided to drop the series in favor of the Indian Head-Buffalo design created by James Fraser. Fraser was a prominent sculptor and his coin seemed to reflect America better than the one in circulation.

The final work on the new nickel was taking longer than expected. The Mint workers became concerned that it might not be possible to have the new coin in production in 1913. As a result, Mint Director George Roberts attempted to calm their fears by issuing a staff memo on December 13, 1912, telling them to "Do nothing about five cent coinage until the new designs are ready for use." That same day the last, legally produced Liberty Head Nickel were struck. They were all dated 1912!

Although the planned coin design had been known for some time, Director Roberts had taken the precaution of ordering dies for a Liberty Head Nickel bearing the 1913 date. The dies, which were produced just in case the Buffalo design was rejected at the last minute, were locked in the vault.

The hubs for the new Indian-Buffalo designs arrived at the Philadelphia Mint on December 26, 1912, and were immediately turned over to the Chief Engraver. However, Director Roberts told Superintendent John H. Landis to take no action regarding the coins until formal approval of the new design had been received.

And so the background for dishonesty had been prepared. The Philadelphia Mint had the materials for producing two entirely different designs of nickels locked in its vaults. No matter which head design was used for the official coinage, it would be possible to privately strike specimens of the other type—specimens which would be worth a small fortune on the open market.

On February 19, 1913, the long-awaited authorization to proceed with the striking of the newly designed coins came through. Two days later production began.

While the Indian-Buffalo Nickels were in preparation, an injunction prohibiting the use of the Liberty Head design kept the 1913 dies in the vault. There are no Mint records indicating that the coin dies were removed or disturbed in any way. However, someone did use them to strike five illegal 1913 specimens of the old style nickels.

Because no one likes to think that the dishonesty which plagued the Mint's early years carried into the twentieth century, there have been several theories expressed concerning the origin of the coins. These have all implied that the coins were legitimately struck and illegitimately removed from the Mint. It is worth looking at these ideas to see why they are not valid.

One theory held that the coins were what is known as "set-up" pieces. When the coiner is setting up the press, he takes impressions to check for both pressure and alignment. The impressions are not full relief and they are inconsistent in relation to each other. These irregular impressions are checked by the die setter, then melted. If the 1913 coins were set-up pieces, they would not have been perfectly struck and consistent in their relief as a study of the five Liberty Head coins reveals them to be.

A second theory has the coins being what were known as die trials. In the early days of the Mint, die trials were struck every few years of a coin's design. By the time the 1913 Liberty Head Nickels were produced the Mint operations had been standardized and die trials were no longer made at regular intervals as they once had been. They were struck only when a new die design was introduced. Die trials had been prepared in the 1880's when the Liberty Head design was created and again for the new Buffalo-Indian coin. But they certainly would not have been made for a coin which had circulated for 30 years.

The only possible explanation is the generally accepted conclusion that the coins were struck for personal gain. It is almost certain that they were struck from the 1913 dies held in the vault. However, it is also possible that there were undated Liberty Head Nickel dies left over from the previous year. It would have been easy to punch in the 1913 date, then use the die for the five coins that were struck. Whichever was the case, the coins were definitely produced without official authorization.

The coins were unknown to the public until December, 1919, when Samuel W. Brown of North Tonawanda, New York, placed an advertisement for them in the magazine *The Numismatist,* the publication of the American Numismatic Association (ANA). He offered to pay $500 apiece for any 1913 Liberty Head Nickel he was sent, preferably in Proof condition. The offer was raised to 600 dollars the following month and he continued his advertising campaign through March, 1920. Then, in August of that year, Brown proudly displayed the "fruits" of his advertisements at the ANA's annual convention. A review of that display appeared in the October issue of *The Numismatist.* It stated:

"Samuel W. Brown of North Tonawanda, New York, was present for a short time on Monday. He had with him a specimen of the latest great rarity in U.S. coinage, the nickel of 1913 of the Liberty Head type. It was among the exhibits of the Convention, with a label announcing that it was valued at $600, which amount Mr. Brown announced he is ready to pay for all Proof specimens offered to him.

"An explanation of its rarity is that at the close of 1912, the Mint authorities not having received orders to use the dies of the Buffalo type nickel at the beginning of 1913, prepared a master die of the Liberty Head type dated 1913, and from this master die a few pieces, believed to be five, in Proof were struck. None of them are believed to have been placed in circulation."

Needless to say, the coins aroused great interest and there was much discussion about their origin. Brown's explanation went unquestioned until someone took the time to check the Mint's records. Not only was his story unsubstantiated by the facts, some interesting information about his background also came to life.

Samuel W. Brown turned out to be a former Mint employee who had been hired by the Philadelphia Mint on December 18, 1903. He served as Assistant Curator of the Mint's coin collection from 1904 through 1907 during which time he learned about the premiums collectors would pay for rare specimens. In April, 1906, he joined the ANA receiving the membership number 808.

Brown was the Mint's storekeeper when he resigned his position on November 14, 1913. He later achieved fame as a U.S. Assay Commissioner, a Mayor of North Tonawanda, and a member of the community's board of education. He died in 1944 at the age of 64, never having changed his story about the origin of the coins.

It is obvious that Brown knew the value of rare coins due to his position at the Mint. He also had complete access to the vaults and could easily have removed the 1913 Liberty Head Nickel dies long enough to either strike them or give them to accomplices for striking. This is the only explanation I have found that can not be disproved and it is the one which I believe is accurate.

It is likely that Brown kept the coins hidden for several years after leaving the Mint so that no one would suspect him of dishonesty or be suspicious when he made his miraculous "discovery" of the coins. When at last he felt certain he was safe, he cleverly advertised for the coins for several months before uncovering not just one, but all five of the coins. What made him suspect their existence in the first place has never been revealed. If he was not in on the striking of the pieces, there is no logical reason why he would have bothered advertising for the coins at all.

The Numismatist for January, 1924, carried another advertisement for the 1913 Liberty Head Nickels, this time announcing their impending sale. The ad had been placed by a Philadelphia dealer named August Wagner. He offered the coins mounted in a black leather case along with a 1913 Buffalo Nickel pattern piece struck in copper. They were sold for a price, reportedly $2,000, to Colonel Edward Howland Robinson Green, an eccentric multi-millionaire whose collection became one of the most outstanding ever assembled.

One of the most interesting aspects of the 1913 Liberty Head Nickels is the fact that no attempt has ever been made to have them returned to the Mint. One of the Mint regulations, established July 1, 1887, reads:

"The emission of impressions of experimental dies, whether in soft metal or in metal of the same weight and fineness proper to coins of the same denomination, is unlawful except in the case of pattern pieces of such denominations of coins as are coined for general circulation during the calendar year of its date.

"All impressions taken in copper, bronze, or other soft metal from an experimental die, are required to be destroyed as soon as the purpose for which it was struck is subserved.

"The above provisions, prescribed by the 'General Instructions and Regulations in Relation to the Transaction of Business at the Mints and Assay Offices of the United States,' approved by the secretary of the Treasury, have been in force since May 14, 1874.

"The striking of a piece in the semblance of a United States coin in a metal or alloy, or of a weight or fineness, other than prescribed by law, is a violation of section 5460 of the Revised Statutes.

"The emission or offer for sale or exchange of an impression from any die of a coin of the United States, or of a proposed coin of the United States, but with a device or devices not authorized by law, whether such die has been prepared at the Mint of the United States or elsewhere, is contrary to the provisions of Section 3517 and 5461, Revised Statutes.

"No impression from any coinage die of the United States struck in other metal than that authorized by law or of a weight and fineness other than prescribed by law (Revised Statutes 3513, 3514, 3515), or pattern piece bearing a legend of a coin of the United States, and bearing a device or devices not authorized by law (Revised Statutes 3516, 3517, vide Mint regulations) should be in existence longer than required for the lawful purpose for which it was authorized to be struck.

"Any emission, for private or personal use or possession, from the Mints of the United States of pieces of the character above specified has been in violation of the coinage laws of the United States."

Other coins, illegally issued after this act was passed, have been confiscated by the Government. One was even taken from the stock of a dealer just prior to an auction sale which was to have featured the coin.

Yet there is no record of Government action to reclaim any of the 1913 coins.

Following Colonel Green's death, the coins were again sold and today the five are in the hands of five different collectors. After a fairly recent sale, when the coin first broke the $100,000 mark, a specimen was featured on the television program *Hawaii Five-O*. Since that time its value has risen to approximately that of the 1804 silver dollar—despite the fact that the coin was illegally produced and has been improperly allowed to remain in collectors' hands.

There is yet another coin which is not known to exist at this writing but which may yet come to light. This is a specimen(s) of the 1964 Peace Type silver dollar.

The Peace Type silver dollar was struck from 1921 through 1935, when silver dollar production ceased in the United States. In 1964, Congressmen from silver producing states began promoting the concept of a new silver dollar, retaining the Peace Design of 40 years earlier. Dies were prepared and specimens struck before the concept was abandoned. All of these coins were supposedly destroyed, but I would not be surprised to one day see someone reveal the existence of one of these coins which just "happened" to escape the security system of the Mint.

12

Dollar of Death

The China of the early 1900s was filled with people living a century behind the rest of the world. For many years the people had been dominated by tyrannical emperors and vicious war lords who felt that an ignorant, superstitious populace would not be much of a threat to their power. Criticism of the government could result in severe punishment.

When the revolution came, led by the famous Dr. Sun Yat-sen, the people were fighting against the cruelty they had known. The concept of building a republic was something few could grasp. They only knew that no form of government could be worse than the one they had been living under.

Republican China came into existence in 1912. The leaders were faced with the Herculean task of building a new country from the old. They needed to organize the people and upgrade their standard of living. This meant changes in medicine, education, and, most important, communication. Dirt paths and mountain trails offered the only approaches from village to village. Travel was difficult and people were isolated from one another. Rapid communication was impossible.

By 1921 only a thousand miles of highways capable of holding automobiles had been built in all of China. The major form of transportation was the wheelbarrow so the typical peasant was not overly concerned. Only in Tsingtao were the roads any good and these had been built by the Germans who vacationed there during the summer. The area was a beautiful port city with resorts and private vacation homes built in the mountains. The roads led from the city to the private residences so, although they were well made, they were of little value to the average Chinese citizen.

Despite the many problems encountered by the owners of automobiles who desired to do much traveling, motor cars were increasingly seen on the streets of Shanghai and other large cities. These vehicles seemed to hold an unusual fascination for the general public. They became the unofficial symbol of the new government.

How much the automobiles meant to the people can be seen in the case of the city of Hangchow. During the revolution an imperial army garrison stationed in the city had been defeated and their barracks destroyed. This left an area of slightly more than one square mile which the republican government had carefully laid out in broad streets to handle automobile traffic. This was done despite the fact that there was not one automobile to be found anywhere in the city. As one native proudly exclaimed, "Well, you wouldn't expect us to buy cars before we had streets broad enough to run them on, would you?"

The Hangchow road building continued with many miles added to the initial construction. However, it was 20 years after the first streets were laid before an automobile was seen in the city.

Some interesting sidelights concerning the road building involved an American soldier, Joseph Stilwell, who would eventually become a four-star general during World War II and the most important American military man in China. He made his first trip to China in 1921, less than a year after a severe famine had devastated the country. The International Relief Committee of the Red Cross took him from his military duties and asked him to serve as their Chief Engineer, building roads in Shansi. Their request made little sense since his engineering training consisted of what little he had been given as a West Point undergraduate. However, he was enthusiastic and agreed to head the proposed four-month project which would involve his living, working, and eating with the construction bosses and laborers.

The reasons for the new road were two-fold. The construction would provide employment for starving refugees and it would improve transportation throughout the area. The latter situation would allow for better distribution of needed food in the future to help prevent a recurrence of massive starvation.

Stilwell's project was to be 82 miles long, linking the Yellow River with Jung-tu. It would be a gravel road 22 feet in width. A total of 6,000 men were engaged in the project which was handled with primitive methods and simple hand tools.

The mayor of Ch'i K'ou, located on the Yellow River, asked that the road pass through his town rather than through a neighboring village as

The Chinese "dollar of death."

originally planned. He knew the road would make his name famous and he was anxious for the publicity.

One of the rest stops for some of the construction workers was an inn about which Stilwell commented, "the courtyard is full of mules, packs and pack-saddles, chickens and pigs . . . The patrons at various plank tables in a single big room crouch over their bowls of noodles, drawing the food into their mouths with the aid of chopsticks and suction . . . The cook dishes out noodle stew from a tremendous iron pot a yard wide, serves it in a bowl which has just been used by a previous customer and which he cleans by wiping with a dark object like a piece of garbage waste. He wipes a pair of chopsticks on his trousers, puts them in the bowl, hands it to a serving boy who presents it with a flourish to the customer."

At another point he had to change the native construction methods. When a bridge was needed, some of the laborers took the wheels off one of their carts, turned the cart upside down and announced that that was the bridge.

In 1926, the most important builder of roads, as far as coin history is concerned, came into power. That was the year that General Chow Hsi-ch'eng became governor of Kweichow.

Kweichow was located in the south of China and had only limited methods of communication and transportation. Any roads which may have existed when General Chow became governor were so small that they went unrecorded.

General Chow inaugurated one of the most ambitious road building programs undertaken to date. The provincial capital of Kweiyang was rebuilt around a massive highway system that linked all areas of the province.

Chow's motives were actually two-fold. He wanted to improve his province, it was true, but he also hoped to increase the highway to the point where he would have quick access to wide areas of China. He wanted to increase his fame and power, hoping, eventually, to gain control of the nation.

In the three short years of his rule, the initial road building program was completed and the immodest General Chow announced the event by ordering a commemorative coin to be struck. The obverse of the coin has a crest surrounded by Chinese figures which translate to the words KWEICHOW SILVER COIN. There is also a circle with the words 17th YEAR

OF MIDDLE FLOWERY REPUBLIC (1928) and ONE YUAN, the equivalent of a dollar.

It is the reverse that is of greatest interest, though. The center of the coin shows a popular make sedan automobile. Surrounding it are Chinese characters which say GOVERNMENT OF KWEICHOW ISSUE and 7 CHIEN . . . 2 FEN.

The automobile rests on what is supposed to be a road over blades of grass. However, if the coin is rotated a quarter turn, and if you have a mind for abstractions, it appears that the blades of grass suddenly take on the appearance of the Chinese symbols for "Si Chen" or Hsi-ch'eng, the governor's name.

Such secret writing was often used on both coins and paper money, but not to commemorate the person who ordered the striking.

The Chinese were outraged by this act of conceit. The soothsayers announced that General Chow would be killed in a violent automobile crash caused by the coin.

In 1929 the predictions came true, though probably not for the reasons the prophets of doom had anticipated. The General was leading some soldiers against an enemy army when he went too far in advance of his troops. The enemy surrounded the car in which he was riding and killed him.

The story of the death appeared in the *New York Herald Tribune* in December, 1933. It stated "Chinese superstition attributes the violent death of General Chow Si-keng (sic), Governor of Kweichow Province from 1926 to 1929, to the minting of a Kweichow silver dollar bearing the design of an automobile. Kweichow Province has no railways, and until Chow's administration had few motor highways. General Chow was an enthusiastic exponent of road building and a few months after his assumption of office compelled the virtual rebuilding of Kweiyang, the provincial capital, by arbitrarily widening all of the city streets and constructing an extensive system of automobile highways.

"To popularize road building, the Kweichow chief executive ordered the minting of a provincial silver dollar stamped on one side with the picture of an automobile. The coin had a standard silver content and was equivalent to the Chinese yuan. But the general's passion for rapid communication was destined to be the indirect cause of his death. During a campaign against a military rival, General Li Shao-yen, the provincial chairman was riding in a motor car at the head of his troops. Too far ahead of his forces, the general's car was surrounded by an enemy advance guard and he was slain.

"Chinese soothsayers, who attribute the death of the Chinese general to the minting of the 'automobile dollar,' have a different explanation of the executive's purpose in designing the new coin. They charge that the provincial chairman wished to have his own profile printed on the face of a new dollar in emulation of Yuan Shih-kai and Sun Yat-sen. Official modesty, however, forbade such a procedure, so the chief executive is said to have hit upon the clever subterfuge. General Chow gave instructions to design a new dollar featuring a motor car in bas relief. That the implication might be unmistakable, the vegetation below the car were so arranged that they formed the characters 'Si-chen,' the personal name of Chow Si-keng.

"It is said that the soothsayers predicted that the provincial chairman would die a violent death in a motor car accident as punishment for his pride and ostentation. General Chow's death was a misfortune to the province because at the time he was engaged in constructing two important truck-line motor roads."

And so ends the story of the dollar of death. Approximately 50,000 were believed struck and, despite its supposed revenge against the General, the coin is among the most popular of all world dollar issues.

13

The United States'
Most Beautiful Coin

United States coinage has never been known for beautiful medallic art. Although some magnificent designs have been proposed to the Mint from time to time over the years, these have been almost universally rejected. Most of the concepts used have been functional at best. And a few, such as the "Silly Head" and "Booby Head" Large Cents, have been downright ridiculous.

In 1905 the majority of the coins in circulation bore designs reflecting the extremely limited ability of their creator, Charles Barber, the Chief Engraver of the United States Mint. If his coins are any indication of his artistic talents, he was a man who was a good technician but he lacked creativity. All his pieces were rather consistent in design, dull, and uninteresting.

The one slight exception was the rather intricate and interesting reverse Barber designed for the Double Eagle ($20 gold piece). However, the obverse for that coin as well as for the other gold pieces was the standard Liberty Head concept. To make matters worse, the gold coins other than the $20 denomination had reverses showing eagles which appeared to be suffering from malnutrition.

The minor coinage was not much better. The Morgan Dollar had shown some originality of design but the Barber coinage was bland and sterile. He seemed concerned only with making functional coins. He either could not conceive them as miniature works of art or was incapable of producing aesthetically pleasing designs.

It is interesting to note that Charles Barber's real interest was not coinage but portraiture. If left on his own as a young man, he probably would have become a portrait artist of note, since his ability to exactly reproduce a person's likeness was his one talent. Unfortunately he was greatly influenced by his father who served as the Mint's Chief Engraver immediately preceding his son's appointment to the position. The father wanted his son, a third generation artist and engraver, to follow in the family tradition and young Barber agreed.

Charles Barber was not a native of the United States. He was born in London in 1840, shortly before the family moved to the United States. He was 29 when he became an assistant engraver at the Philadelphia Mint. He attained the position of Chief Engraver after his father's death in 1880.

Barber's greatest works all involved portraiture. He prepared designs for medals for Presidents Arthur and Garfield, as well as working on the Great Seal Of The United States and the Indian Peace Medals.

Barber's ideas for coinage were extremely limited. He was quite content with a simple Liberty Head design that was easily executed and produced, but visually dull. Coins were meant for business purposes so he saw no reason to expend any great artistic endeavor on them. To make matters worse, he was an extremely jealous man who could not stand the idea of other designers preparing U.S. coins. He acted as though he felt inferior and had to reinforce his position at the Mint by tearing down the efforts of any other artists. He had the habit of rejecting outsider's coin designs for one reason or another, usually they were quite petty. He went so far as to want to personally alter the popular Lincoln Cent design because Victor David Brenner, the artist who created it, had placed his initials on the coin. In that fight Barber ignored the fact that his own initials appeared on the design for the dime the Mint struck from 1892 to 1916.

Fortunately for numismatics, 1905 was also a year in which Theodore Roosevelt was President. Roosevelt was a great student of art history who was especially fond of the ancient Greek coin designs. He lacked knowledge of the technical aspects of coin production but felt certain that the appearance of the American coins could be improved with more intricate detail and higher relief.

While Roosevelt's mind was on changes in coinage, the famous artist Augustus Saint-Gaudens was in Washington to create the Roosevelt Inauguration Medal which would be sculpted by his pupil, Adolf Weinman. Saint-Gaudens was a world renowned artist who had last done work for the Government in 1891. That year he had been asked to judge a public competition for new coinage designs. The judging led to a request that he design the medal for the 1892 Columbian Exposition. However, Saint-Gaudens soon learned that the medal design would have to be a joint effort. Charles Barber was not about to let someone else be the sole creator of a medal to be produced by the Mint. Barber would handle the reverse as well as making suggestions about the "proper" obverse design.

Saint-Gaudens was disgusted by the restrictions under which he was forced to work. He realized that no one in the Government had the courage to thwart the Chief Engraver's desires, even though he had originally been assured that the design would be his total creation. When Saint-Gaudens complained, he was told, in effect, that the wishes of the Chief Engraver were law. He had to either cooperate or forget the commission.

Roosevelt and Saint-Gaudens were immediately impressed with one another. Saint-Gaudens liked Roosevelt's independence and was pleased by the President's appreciation of art. Roosevelt saw in Saint-Gaudens a man who was capable of designing the type of coins he felt a great nation should have—coins that would be similar to ancient pieces such as the Greek gold coins of Alexander the Great.

As the two men came to know each other better, Roosevelt asked the designer about the possibility of making some new coins which would be of high relief with raised rims. He said the artist would have complete freedom though he wanted Saint-Gaudens to follow the Greek methods of design.

Saint-Gaudens agreed but had some reservations. In a letter to Roosevelt dated November 11, 1905, he said, in part, ". . . Of course the great coins (and you might say the only coins) are the Greek ones you speak of, just as the great medals are those of the fifteenth century by Pisani and Sperandie. Nothing would please me more than to make the attempt in the direction of the heads of Alexander, but the authorities on modern monetary requirements would I fear 'throw fits' to speak emphatically if the thing were done now. It would be great if it could be accomplished, and I do not see what objection would be if the edges were high enough to prevent the rubbing. Perhaps an inquiry from you would not receive the antagonistic reply from those who have the say in such matters that would certainly be made to me.

"Up to the present I have done no work on the actual model for the coins, but have made sketches, and the matter is constantly on my mind.

I have about determined on the composition of one side, which would contain an eagle very much like the one I placed on your medal with a modification that would be advantageous; on the other side some kind of a (possibly winged) figure of Liberty striding forward as if on a mountain top, holding aloft on one arm a shield bearing the stars and stripes with the word Liberty marked across the field; in the other hand perhaps a flaming torch, the drapery would be flowing in the breeze. My idea is to make it a living thing and typical of progress."

Roosevelt agreed to intercede for Saint-Gaudens. He said he would try to convince the Mint or, more precisely, Charles Barber, that the coins should be struck with rims that were raised somewhere between existing coinage and the Greek designs. He said the thickness would have to be controlled to prevent bankers from complaining when they had to stack the gold for counting.

Saint-Gaudens was originally supposed to work on three coin designs including a ten dollar gold piece (Eagle) and a one cent coin, in addition to the Double Eagle. Under Federal law the head of Liberty had to appear on the coins so Roosevelt suggested that an Indian headdress might be used on the Liberty figure. He felt it was more distinctive than the Phrygian cap which was a Roman device adopted on many American coins over the years.

Roosevelt was practical enough to warn Saint-Gaudens that a certain amount of change from the original Greek style would be necessary. If the coins were too thick, bankers would object to the difficulty of handling them. He said they should have raised figures and raised rims, though not so high as on the unstackable Greek coins.

Roosevelt also wanted to break with tradition by removing the words "In God We Trust" from the coins even though they had appeared on all designs used since the 1860's. He felt it was wrong to use the name of the Lord on so commercial an object as a coin. He asked Saint-Gaudens to remove the motto after checking and discovering that it was not required by law. Saint-Gaudens agreed, though in 1908, the second year the coins were in circulation, Congress passed a law which forced the addition of the motto on all current and future coins.

Roosevelt was impressed with Saint-Gauden's preliminary sketches for the coins and enjoyed remarking about how much he disliked the Mint's lack of creativity on its past products. He said, "I think it will seriously increase mortality among the employees of the Mint at seeing such a desecration, but they will perish in a good cause. Whatever I produce cannot be worse than the inanities now displayed on our coins, and we will at least have made an attempt in the right direction, and serve the country by increasing the mortality at the Mint." He also jokingly referred to the coins he was having designed as "my crime."

By June, 1906 the coins were almost ready to be produced on a trial basis. Saint-Gaudens wrote to Roosevelt, "The eagle side of the gold piece is finished and is undergoing innumerable experiments with reduction . . .

"Now I am attacking the cent. It may interest you to know that on the 'Liberty' side of the cent I am using a flying eagle; a modification of the device which was used on the cent of 1857. I had not seen that coin for many years and was so impressed by it that I thought if carried out with some modifications, nothing better could be done. It is by all odds the best design on any American coin." He arranged to have dies made in Paris which would reproduce a coin as detailed as his original work.

"These models are simply immense—if such a slang way of talking is permissible in reference to giving a modern nation one coinage at least which shall be as good as that of the ancient Greeks," Roosevelt commented after receiving them. "I have instructed the Director of the Mint that these dies are to be reproduced just as quickly as possible and just as they are. It is simply splendid. I suppose I shall be impeached for it in Congress but I shall regard that as a very cheap payment."

Saint-Gaudens would be doing little more work on the coins. He had completed numerous obverse sketches for both the Eagle and Double Eagle as well as 70 sketches of the reverse. But he was dying of cancer and the physical modeling of the coins had to be turned over to his assistant, Henry Hering. He was no longer strong enough to complete the work himself.

Hering was unfamiliar with coin production methods and did not know what type of model to make. He decided to make a plaster $20 gold piece nine inches across that was as high in a relief as he thought could be achieved when made into a die. He knew that it would take more than one striking to produce a coin from his model, but he felt that by comparing coins bearing different numbers of strikes he would be able to develop a practical design for the final coin.

Saint-Gaudens distrusted Charles Barber and was certain Barber would do what he could to alter or reject the design. He told Hering to use the Paris Mint for the reductions. He said that once the reductions were approved, they would be returned to France "where the die can properly be made."

Roosevelt was becoming impatient. Too much time was passing without the coins being completed. He ordered Mint Director George Roberts to make the reductions of the Double Eagle and asked that Saint-Gaudens forward the models at once. This was done, much to Roosevelt's delight.

When Hering had to meet Barber, their encounter went as he had expected. He later wrote of the incident: "I took the model to the Philadelphia Mint and was introduced by the Director to Mr. Barber, who was the Chief Engraver. When he saw the plaster model of the $20 gold piece, which was about nine inches in diameter, he rejected it and said it was impossible for any mint to coin it. I told him my reasons for doing it and that we would have to experiment. After considerable discussion, he finally decided to make the die.

"In the meantime, I returned to the studio and made another model much lower in relief. I had about finished with the second model when the Mint informed that the die of the first model was ready for experiment. I immediately went to Philadelphia carrying the second and revised model with me. When I showed it to Mr. Barber, it was no more practical than the first model, and he refused to have anything to do with it. However, we went to the press room to see how the experimental die of the first model would work out; so a circular disc of gold was placed in the die and by hydraulic pressure of 172 tons, I think it was, we had our first stamping, and the impression showed a little more than one-half of the modeling. I had them make a cast of this for my guidance. The coin was again placed on the die for another strike and again it showed a little more of the modeling, and so it went, on and on until the ninth strike when the coin showed up in every detail. This coin I took to show Mr. St. Gaudens, who in turn sent it to the President, and I think Mrs. Theodore Roosevelt still has it. I do not know of any more being struck, as we had finished with that die."

Hering's account is not quite accurate since there were apparently two coins struck from the original die. The coin given to Roosevelt was eventually housed in the museum built to honor him. A second coin remained in the Saint-Gaudens' estate and was housed by the American Numismatic Society.

The original coin was a combination of ideas which eventually were found on the high relief and lettered edge coins released into circulation in 1907. Liberty's face was fuller than she appeared on the circulating high relief coin, and her skirt folds were not so detailed as they would later appear. In general she was slightly larger and had less detailed work than the circulating pieces. The Roman numerals used on the high relief coin appeared on the sample, but there was less of an edge than there would be on the low relief coin.

On the reverse, the eagle's left wing is raised slightly more than would be the case on the circulating high relief coin. Its appearance was one of greater depth.

Hering had casts made of the various samplings and showed the work to Barber. Again Barber claimed the relief was too great for reproduction and would have to be reduced. Hering had expected the criticism and was happy to accede to the Chief Engraver's wishes.

The major problem at the Mint was that the coining equipment was as out-dated as Barber's thinking. The machine used for reduction was inferior to what had been developed abroad. When Hering returned with a new model for the Double Eagle, the subsequent Mint reductions were horrible. Hering later wrote:

"I examined the reduction of my model, which seemed to me very poor. Mr. Barber claiming it could not be done better. It just so happened that during my student days in Paris, France, there lived a sculptor named Janvier who invented a reducing machine which was perfection and the French government and, in fact, all the other European goverments, installed Janvier's machine in their mints. So it occurred to me to look over the machine the U.S. Mint was using.

"It was a machine about forty years old and consequently very much out of date. I told Mr. Barber so, but it made no impression on him, so I made my report to Mr. St. Gaudens who in turn told the President. Of course, you can imagine what Teddy's feelings were on hearing the U.S.A. was so much out of date. The outcome was an early visit to the Mint to see another reduction, this time of the $10 gold coin. This Mr. Barber showed me with great glee and after looking it over, I found it also a very poor reduction, whereupon Mr. Barber informed me that it had been done by the Janvier machine, which the Philadelphia Mint had installed."

Hering became angry. He commented that even the best machines fail to work properly when the person running them does not know what he is doing. He did not mention to Barber that he had personally obtained

The Saint-Gaudens $20 gold piece, generally considered to be America's most beautiful coin.

three reductions of the same models from Mr. Janvier, and that they were perfect.

In May, 1907 the Mint workers reported what looked like another setback. To produce coins of properly high relief, several strikes would be necessary, a situation which was not conducive to large scale coinage. Roosevelt notified Saint-Gaudens of this turn of events, asking him to come to the Mint to work out an alteration. However, Saint-Gaudens was dying. He did not know the seriousness of his condition at the time, but he did recognize that he had become too weakened to travel.

Saint-Gaudens died in August, before Hering was able to complete the new models for the Double Eagle. His death was upsetting to the proponents of the new coins. They were anxious to get them into production and feared a setback with the designer gone.

The dies were delivered on September 28 at which time Barber followed his usual procedure and rejected them as being too high a relief. He explained his decision to the superintendent in a long letter that said, in part: "In regard to the double-eagle, my fear now is that before I can reduce the relief on many sudden high points of the design sufficiently to coin, the portions that are already low will be lost and all detail will have disappeared.

"That it will ever be satisfactory I cannot say, though I have very grave doubts. From the first time that this change of design in our gold coins was proposed, I have tried to impress upon the mind of Mr. Saint-Gaudens' representative, the absolute necessity of low relief models for coinage, and until proper suitable models are furnished, there can be no certainty that there will be any satisfactory results."

Roosevelt had waited long enough. The coins were a dream he had cherished. It was already too late for the designer to share the joy of seeing that dream turned into reality. He decided that the coins had to go into production, immediately. The Mint should use the hydraulic presses to make as many impressions as were necessary to produce each coin in sufficiently high relief. He said that for all he cared, they could take all day to make one coin, but they were to begin making those coins at once.

The strikings which resulted from the go-ahead order were both beautiful and unusual. The early coins had no border, so when several strikes were made with the hydraulic press, the metal that would normally have flowed into the borders was forced between the collar and the die, creating a high wire edge. When they were issued in December, the banks complained that it was impossible to stack them.

Barber had done the President's bidding, but it was time for his ego to reassert itself. He altered the third pair of Double Eagle models Hering had made, reducing relief, replacing the Roman date with Arabic numerals and destroying much of the detail and beauty the coins had had. There was much criticism of his unauthorized action, but the altered coins were adopted. Even the proponents of the original design admitted that the coins could not have been produced through conventional methods and Congress was not about to continue paying the high cost of having coins stamped several times each by the hydraulic press.

Hering felt the Saint-Gaudens' coins had been deliberately sabotaged by Barber. He believed that a combination of Barber's jealousy, untrained workers using the new Janvier machine, and the haste with which changes were made resulted in the banks' stacking problems. He felt that the high relief coins should have been practical for wide-scale production and was quite frustrated by what happened.

President Roosevelt was delighted with the new Double Eagles. In a reply to a friend's favorable comment about them, he wrote: "I am very much pleased that you like that coin. I shall have all kinds of trouble over it: but I do feel that what you say is true, that is, that it is the best coin that has been struck for two thousand years, and that no matter what is its temporary fate, it will serve as a model for future coin makers, and that eventually the difficulties in connection with making such coins will be surmounted. I had a hundred thousand of them struck before Congress could get to me, which they did on the score of expense, and the subsequent coins are not as good as the first issue . . ."

Roosevelt's enthusiasm for the Saint-Gaudens' coinage has been repeated by many others. Despite the best efforts of the jealous Charles Barber, the coins remain the most beautiful ever to come out of the United States Mint.

14

The Unusual Story of the Lincoln Cent

The lowly Lincoln Cent hardly seems capable of arousing passionate emotions. The simple design, unchanged since 1909, is hardly noticed by the average person. The coin fits in a parking meter rather nicely, at least those meters which have not been converted for nickels or dimes. But for other than utilitarian uses, who really cares about the coin? No one today. Yet surprisingly, when it was introduced, the nation went insane trying to obtain a specimen. In fact, over the years it has proved to be the most popular coin the United States ever produced.

1909 was a rather unusual year in American history. Slavery had been abolished for more than 50 years but the Ku Klux Klan was extremely strong and growing in popularity. Klansmen had great influence in business and government, their hate seemingly condoned by Congress. That is why it came as such a surprise to minority groups and liberals when the Mint announced a coin would be struck in honor of Abraham Lincoln.

The news of the Lincoln Cent was greeted with joy in the nation's ghettoes. It was called the "coin of freedom" and the "emancipation coin."

With the elation there was also trepidation. A cynical public decided that the new coin would not be a regular issue but rather a short-lived commemorative designed to halt mounting criticism of Government inaction over racial discrimination. People felt the coin would be removed from circulation almost as soon as it was released. They felt that if they did not obtain one when it first appeared, there would be no chance of finding one in the future.

August 2, 1909, was the official first day of issue. Twenty-five million coins had been struck, then divided among the sub-treasuries in New York, Chicago, Philadelphia, Boston, and St. Louis. Within three days the coins had vanished into the hands of the public.

In New York, the Wall Street sub-treasury was mobbed the day of issue. Ten policemen were sent to the scene to maintain order but were quickly overwhelmed by the crowds. Reinforcements arrived but they could do little. In all, New Yorkers took home 700,000 of the new cents which they hid away, made into jewelry, or carried as lucky pieces.

On August 6, with signs reading "NO MORE LINCOLN PENNIES" appearing at all the outlets for the coins, the profiteers began selling whatever they had managed to obtain. Newsboys, street vendors, and others offered their cents to the highest bidders. They further boosted the price by spreading rumors that not only would there be no more coins struck, the ones that had been issued would soon be re-called.

But the Lincoln Cent was not to be short lived. Over 100 million were struck that first year alone and the joy which greeted the coins those first few days was matched by the contempt for the design, held by many in the weeks that followed.

The Lincoln Cent had been designed by the talented artist Victor D. Brenner who came to the United States from Russia in 1880. He was 19 years old and filled with hope. He supported himself by selling matches on New York street corners while attending art classes at night. Later he was able to journey to Paris for training as a sculptor. By the time he was 38 he had been involved in the creation of several designs for medals for the United States Government.

The Lincoln coin actually had its origin as a medal. It was the summer of 1908 and Charles Eliot Norton had given Brenner a photograph of Lincoln to help the artist prepare a plaque and medal for the 100th anniversary of the great leader's birthday. His mind was on the assignment while he was busy sketching President Theodore Roosevelt whose portrait would be appearing on a Panama Canal Service Medal.

Brenner and Roosevelt began talking about coins and Brenner suggested Lincoln be honored on a new issue. The President was enthusiastic about the idea and asked Brenner to submit some designs for possible approval.

Brenner's enthusiasm for the Lincoln coin was not the result of personal interest in Lincoln's life. Rather he was fascinated by the artistic possibilities in so distinctive a face, and anxious to begin the project.

The Lincoln medal was artistically rewarding but, to Brenner, it was just a likeness, devoid of life. He wanted the bust shown on the coin to be so perfectly sculpted that a viewer would feel himself in the presence of Lincoln.

The first sketches for the new coin were submitted on January 18, 1909. The obverse, naturally, was the head of Lincoln. But the reverse was copied from a coin Brenner had seen while studying abroad—the French Two Franc piece. One sketch showed a leafy twig with "1 CENT" over it. Surrounding this were the words UNITED STATES OF AMERICA 1908. The second coin showed a walking woman, representing Liberty, carrying some leaves in one hand and a scroll in the other. The date was split by her body and surrounding her were the words "UNITED STATES OF AMERICA."

Brenner's design was intended for a half dollar, not a cent, but he would not be allowed to prepare such a coin. Chief Engraver Charles Barber was already creating designs for larger denomination coins. Only the cent and the nickel were available for an "outsider" to change.

The use of the French Franc design for the reverse also caused Brenner trouble. If the Liberty design was adopted it was felt that there might be a question of legality. "This figure is supposed to symbolize Liberty, and to use it, it seems to me, would destroy our license to use the Lincoln head, so much desired, on the obverse side. The law does not provide for two impressions or figures emblematic of Liberty. Then, as this is the simplest coin we have it seems to me it should call for the plainest and most distinct design," wrote the Mint Director to the Secretary of the Treasury after reviewing Brenner's ideas.

Brenner decided against arguing over the counters to his design. He was an artist with a commission. It was essential he please his client provided his basic concept, the Lincoln obverse, was not changed. He submitted a plan for a different reverse design and was shortly contacted by Barber. The Chief Engraver was concerned with the way the design would reproduce. He wanted to explain the technical difficulties of stamping a coin which required some flexibility on the part of the designer.

Barber said that upon examining the proposed Lincoln model, he found that "the field in front of the face is one plane while the field at the back of the head is an entirely different plane. This you will see will never do as we have to finish the field of the dies mechanically in order to comply with the wish of the Director, namely to have the field finished smooth and one radius."

Barber explained that the final sketch of the coin should avoid having bold sections of design opposite each other on the two faces. He said that he could not give specific advice on the relief of the design without seeing the finished product, however. He suggested that previous coins be used as models when trying to determine how much of the design should be raised.

Finally Barber stressed, "In designing for a coin you must give due weight to the mechanical requirements of coinage and remember that great quantities of coins are demanded against time, and therefore, everything that can be done to simplify both the making of the dies and the production of the coin, must be considered."

At last the design was completed. Plaster models were made and, in a touch of artistic egotism, Brenner signed his full name to the obverse of the coin, an action that would not be tolerated. A kind but firm note informed Brenner that the models were perfect though his signature would have to be removed. Only initials placed unobtrusively on the reverse would be permitted. Brenner complied.

The reductions of the approved plaster bust were made and approved by everyone involved with the production. The coin was authorized on July 14 with issue tentatively set for August 4.

After such a long, behind-the-scenes battle for the proper design, it would seem that the Lincoln Cent would be above artistic criticism. However, this was not to be the case. The news media was overwhelmed with the audacity of a designer who would place his initials on a coin. The anti-Roosevelt New Orleans *Picayune* saw the initials as a Roosevelt plot and called them "The first visible and outward emblem of the transmogrification of the republic into an empire."

The Rochester *Post Express* was equally indignant though for other reasons. "Never before in all our coinage have the initials of the designers appeared on a coin. If one designer may put one initial on a coin, and the next put on three initials, the next will want his whole name to appear, and if on coins, why not logically on postage stamps, greenbacks, and bonds." Of course, the editorial writer did not know that Brenner had wanted his full name to appear, for if he had, his words might have been even more heated. He was also ignorant of numismatics as an editorial in *The Numismatist* would explain.

The editorial read: "The name of the designer, or artist, appearing on coin types is as old as art in metal. The signed coined types of Kimon, Eukleides, and others of the period of finest art, B.C. 405–345, are examples which artists of late days have striven to emulate. Signed coin types and marks to identify the designer are to be found on the metal money of all periods and particularly of today.

"Of the coins of the United States, we find the beautiful pattern cent of 1792, bearing the name BIRCH; the dollars of 1836, C. GOBRECHT, and the Lafayette-Washington dollars have BARTLETT, in script, at the base of the equestrian statue. The Liberty head type $20 gold piece, coined from 1849 to 1907, has J.B.L. on the base of the neck of Liberty —for the designer J.B. Longacre, who also designed the Indian head cent which has just been discontinued and which bears his mark, on both obverse and reverse for the designer, Mint Engraver George T. Morgan. Our present type of silver coins has a B for Charles E. Barber, the Mint's chief engraver, as has also the Columbian half-dollar. Saint-Gaudens' design $20 gold piece prominently bears his monogram; and B.L.P. is to be found on the Bigelow-Pratt type $2½ and $5, for the artist, Bella L. Pratt.

"With the removal of the initials from the Lincoln cent, our only coins now being struck that do not have marks to indicate the designer are the cent, the five-cent, and the $10 gold pieces. The absence of marks on the $10 gold piece is said to have been an omission which would not have occurred had Saint-Gaudens lived."

On August 5, coin production was stopped. Barber was ordered to Washington to remove the initials and find a way to place an inconspicuous "B" for "Brenner" somewhere on the coin.

A change of the initials was not an easy action. The addition of the letter "B" would be no problem, but the removal of the VDB would require die tooling that would take 14 days. However an immediate end to the problem could be obtained by adding nothing and the erasing of VDB from the hub.

Barber was an extremely jealous man who had resented the use of an outside designer for the creation of the new coin. He had kept his feelings somewhat hidden during the initial creation of the coin, but after the newspaper criticism he let his true attitude come forth. He said that all initials should be removed from the coin. Initials had never been used in full, he said, ignoring St. Gaudens and Pratt who had their initials on the gold pieces. And the single letter "B" should also not be used, he added, because people might think it was another Barber creation, an association he would not tolerate.

Brenner was naturally upset with the changes in his coin. He wanted his initials on the cents. His ego had already been damaged by unauthorized changes in the coin which separated the bust of Lincoln from the edge of the cent. He had designed the obverse so that the bust and the edge would merge. This would have hindered the proper production of the reverse according to Barber. However, the fact that the change was made without consulting Brenner indicates it was probably just the jealous Chief Engraver's way of insuring that he would have a hand in the coin design.

Further complications arose because Brenner's idea for the thickness of the coin was greater than the previous designs. This meant that either a change in the dies had to be made or the vending machines utilizing cents would have to be altered. Naturally Barber was quick to gossip about his latest problem with any government official who would listen. He stressed that such problems were inevitable whenever a designer was used who did not understand coin production. In other words, anyone but Barber was a poor choice.

But the scare tactics proved meaningless. The slight modification necessary for the vending machine coin detectors was easily made. Rather than having the Mint make new dies and hubs to reduce the thickness of the new coins, the machine owners retooled their products. They were quite happy to make the inexpensive alterations to insure the continued use of their machines.

In February, 1917, Barber died. The coinage controversy was buried with him. The full initials of the designer were added to the shoulder of Lincoln, a location the late chief engraver had once said would prove too complicated. It took eight years but Brenner was finally placated.

There was yet another problem with the Lincoln Cent, this one occurring during World War II. The Mint was faced with a shortage of copper. It had originally been used for America's least valued coins because it was an almost worthless metal found in abundance, but as new uses for the metal were found, the price rose dramatically. The demands of war further added to the cost and the Mint was forced to seek an alternative material for use in cents. By the end of 1942 the Mint had actually produced some trial coins of a material which would have shocked the nation if the news was known: the Lincoln Cents were made of plastic!

This story began with the typical problems faced by a nation at war. The men fighting on the front lines had top priority when it came to food, clothing, and material. People back in the United States were expected to make sacrifices for the military in order to ensure the nation's total victory.

The once worthless copper was essential for war and military purposes. Coinage, although important, was still a secondary priority. It was decided that it would be necessary to find an alternate substance to use for the production of the Lincoln Cents. This could not be done without Congressional authorization, however, and Congress temporarily had more important matters on its mind than the production of America's least valued coin.

Mint officials took matters into their own hands. They illegally began seeking a substitute for the copper. Durability, color, weight, and a hundred other factors were considered as metal after metal was analyzed. Some proved too brittle. Others bent with heavy use. Still others which seemed perfect had to be discarded when it was learned they would be needed in the manufacture of new weapons. Everything imaginable was tried. Glass looked good but it shattered. Then plastic was used and, surprisingly enough, it appeared to be the answer; it was stronger than glass and would not shatter into knife-like pieces.

Officially the plastic cent did not exist. It could not be discussed because the experimentation was illegal. Rumors about the new coins were denied. Finally a specimen of the plastic cent, a trial piece, was discovered being used as a toy by the child of an employee of the Durex Plastic & Chemical Corporation of North Tonawanda, New York. The coin was brittle, easily broken with the slightest pressure. It seemed to be only a toy and that is what offiicials would have liked the public to think it was. The coin was actually one of several trial pieces prepared for the Mint during efforts to find the right formula for a durable plastic coinage.

It wasn't until 1943 that the Mint Director finally publicly admitted to experiments with plastic cents. She stated that the few coins which had been produced were struck under controlled conditions in the presence of two officials. These coins had been destroyed a short time later. She also claimed that no serious thought had been given to producing the coins since the War Production Board had determined that the composition of the plastic included materials that would eventually be essential for the war effort.

The Mint Director was only telling part of the story. The Treasury Department had quietly expanded its authority in the field of coinage without Congressional authorization. To admit the full extent of the plans for plastic cents would have been admitting to illegal operations. In reality, the purchase of the Watertown Plastics Corporation and the Waterbury Button Company had been contemplated in order to have a means for producing the plastic coins. In addition, plastic coins were being produced in some quantity, with the first dies reaching the Mint in mid-September, 1942. The coins were struck in varying thicknesses so that the Mint could determine which would wear most effectively.

Congress recognized the need to alter the metal of the Lincoln Cent, but the actions it took came long after the Mint officials had begun their private enterprise. In December, 1942, New York Senator Robert Wagner introduced bill S. 2889 to "further the war effort by authorizing the substitution of other materials for strategic metals used in minor coinage, to authorize the forming of worn and uncurrent standard silver dollars into bars, and for other purposes, and I ask unanimous consent in connection with this bill that a memorandum may be printed in the record."

The bill was fairly extensive, but a summary was made by New York Congressman Sommers of the House Committee on Coinage, Weights, and Measures, which also considered the legislation. He said: "The purpose of this bill is to conserve the metals required for war-production purposes which are now used in minor coins. The bill will permit the minting of minor coins in the denominations of one cent and three cents, which coins shall be of such metallic or other contents, weight, denominations, shape, and limitations of form and design as the Secretary of the Treasury by regulation may prescribe. In determining those physical properties the Secretary of the Treasury is directed to take into consideration the use of these coins in coin-operated devices. The authority contained in this bill is limited to the period between the date of enactment and December 31, 1946." The bill also requested that a million dollar limit be placed on the amount of material which could be purchased for the production of the new coins.

Sommers made his remarks to the House on December 10, 1942, many days after the Mint had begun making plastic coins. The bill had been studied, modified, and passed by financial experts, but had not gone into effect. The plastic coin production which was taking place was, for the moment, illegal.

The fact that the Congressmen were not familiar with Mint experimentation becomes more apparent when studying the conversations of the Congressmen. Discussion revealed that the only control over the Treasury Secretary that had been enacted was a move which prevented him from altering the metallic content of the five cent piece. There were millions of nickel-operated vending machines around the country which could not be retooled to handle a change in the metallic content of the nickels. Such a change would probably prevent the coins from triggering the machines' operating mechanisms, a fact which would make the machines obsolete and cripple the industry. This was the only check Congress had bothered to make on the Treasury Secretary's powers as related to the Mint operations.

One of the Congressmen asked Sommers for specifics regarding the contemplated change in metal content for the cents. He replied, "It is contemplated at present time that they will be made of steel with a zinc coating." He stressed that it would be strictly a temporary measure.

During the debate there was intensive questioning of Sommers concerning the intrinsic value of minor coins. There was concern that alterations in metal would make minor coins worthless.

Sommers pointed out that the present copper coins were practically worthless. The metal first became highly valued when it was needed for the war effort—a temporary demand. Copper had never had much value away from the battlefield.

Ohio's Congressman Smith asked about an alloy of steel which might be used for cents. It was at this point that the Congressmen received their first information concerning Mint experimentation of any sort.

Sommers replied, "let me simply restate what the Mint told me. They said, 'When it first became apparent that we would have a shortage of copper, we immediately experimented with other materials.' They went to zinc because zinc is rather popular for similar coinage in other countries. They had just about completed their experiments with zinc and had brought a bill to my committee when the War Production Board said to them, 'Gentlemen, zinc is now on the critical list.'

"From that they went to plastics. They did some experimentation with plastics and found that they went to the critical list.

"They think now that the metal most readily obtainable at the moment, the easiest to handle, and the one that we can get the quickest, is steel. Consequently, they decided that they would use steel for the period of this bill, coating the steel with zinc for the purpose of protection, and use that for the penny and the three-cent piece."

There were backroom sessions following the open floor debate. During these meetings the Congressmen were less inclined to gentlemanly behavior and heated arguments occurred. It was obvious that there were legal questions concerning the Mint's experimentation because existing legislation did not allow for such private enterprise. Although greatly angered, the Congressmen felt themselves unable to enter into an investigation of Mint officials' actions for possible criminal violations. There were just too many other priorities during wartime. They were also convinced that officials had lied about the destruction of trial pieces, but again the war prevented further investigation.

And so the tale of the plastic cent came to a close—sort of. The Mint stopped producing the cents and Congress did not bother to examine the conduct of the Mint officials. However, the coins, mostly lead colored and apparently made of a plastic composed of cotton flock, powdered minerals, and a bending resin, remained to some degree undestroyed. Pieces may have been given to directors of the plant where they were made, Mint officials, and other dignitaries involved with production. Whatever happened, the coins periodically appear in dealers' hands and are always interesting conversation pieces.

The Lincoln Cent is almost worthless today and is generally ignored, but this lowliest of American coins was once the subject of heated passions, the likes of which have seldom been encountered in the history of United States numismatics.

15

America's "Obscene" Coin

It was a period when women were attacking the puritanical restrictions of the Victorian era: many of them had abandoned the corset and the petticoat; others demanded the right to vote; still others were smoking in public, drinking in hotel bars, or driving the new automobiles! The more daring even took up flying and some, like Emma Goldman, a Greenwich Village anarchist, insisted that the sexual double standard should be ended. If men could have affairs before marriage, she said, women should be given the same privilege—without being accused of immorality.

For years a woman's place had been in the home, but suddenly this ideal was changing. Women, often pressed by poverty and with the desire to win a better life for their families, entered the business world. They were employed in dress shops, offices, factories, and numerous other trades. They were scorned by most, pitied by many, and admired by a few. The *New York American* carried the observations of an anonymous British writer who commented: "About the average American woman of the middle classes there can be no doubt at all. She is incomparably the smartest, most elegant, and beautiful thing that exists under Heaven. It is not of the women of fashion I speak, though many are lovely enough. It is the ordinary, every-day-go-to-work-girl who takes her lunch at Child's, runs to catch a trolley-car, jostles you in the subway, and patronizes what you call the cinematograph theatre and she calls the 'movies.' It is, in fact, the goddess of the typewriter, the fairy of the newspaper office, the grace of the telephone that I sing."

The ideal woman of the editor of the *Ladies' Home Journal* was described in verse: "She is gentle, she is shy; But there's mischief in her eye, She's a flirt."

But even with the new liberalism, American women were considered

delicate creatures to be cared for and protected. For example, fashion-
able dresses were long, high necked, and so tight around the ankles that
walking was difficult. A clergyman commented, "Never in history were
the modes so abhorrently indecent as they are today." Yet the most
innovative design was a dress that imitated the style of a Salvation Army
uniform. Hemlines had climbed higher but ankles were hidden by high
button shoes. A few skirts were of the see-through variety, but all one
saw were their thick, patterned linings.

The Best Seller List reflected the public attitudes. In 1916 Booth
Tarkington's book *Seventeen* captured national acclaim. In it he told
how it was "to be a boy, and seventeen, and in love, and to have a small
sister Jane who eats bread spread with apple sauce."

There was pornography, of course, but it was for men only; women
were creatures of purity and innocence who had to be protected from
the seamier side of life. That is why it came as such a shock to the nation
when the United States Government released coinage that was, according to its critics, *obscene*.

There was never an intention to create an obscene coin, of course.
The Government certainly did not have this in mind when, in 1916, the
Treasury Department held a competition for some new coin designs.
The Charles Barber coinage, mediocre at best, had ended its useful life.
There was a need for new dimes, quarters, and half dollars. Artists were
requested to submit their ideas with the final selection to be made by
joint decision of the Treasury and the Commission of Fine Arts.

A. A. Weinman was selected to handle the dime and the half dollar,
both of which were uncontroversial. The man in whom we are interested
is Hermon A. MacNeil, designer of the Standing Liberty Quarter, America's only "obscene" coin.

The Mint Director was delighted with MacNeil's quarter dollar when
it was first introduced. In the 1916 annual Mint Report, the Director
said, in part: "The design of the 25-cent piece is intended to typify in a
measure the awakening interest of the country to its own protection.

"The law specified that on the obverse of the coin not only the word
'Liberty' but a representation of Liberty shall be shown. In the new
design Liberty is stepping forward to the gateway of the country, and on
the wall are inscribed the words 'In God We Trust,' which words also
appear on the new half dollar, mentioned above. The left arm of the
figure of Liberty is upraised, bearing the shield in the attitude of protection, from which the covering is being drawn. The right hand bears the

olive branch of peace. On the field above the head is inscribed the word 'Liberty,' and on the step under her feet '1916.' The reverse of this coin necessitates by law a representation of the American eagle, and is here shown in full flight, with wings extended, sweeping across the coin. Inscription: 'United States of America' and 'E Pluribus Unum' and 'Quarter Dollar' below. Connecting the lettering above an outer circle are thirteen stars."

To the casual observer, and in this category we must, at least at first, include the Mint Director, the MacNeil design was beautiful.

After years of the dull Charles Barber pieces, the nation was finally getting distinctive medallic art. Even more important, the coin seemed to symbolize the changing mood of the American people who were being drawn into a war in Europe more or less against their will.

Even the model for the coin seemed perfect for the times. Her name was Dora Doscher. She was 22 years old and 5 feet 4½ inches tall, according to newspaper accounts. She had been a sickly child but had developed into a beautiful woman who was a trained nurse, a scenario writer, and a lecturer. She joined the Red Cross as soon as the First World War seemed inevitable. She had also served as the model for the Karl Bitter statue "Diana" which was in the Metropolitan Museum of Art and was the model for Bitter's Pulitzer Memorial Fountain in New York City.

A newspaper article of the day, written by Marguerite Norse, said, in part:

"Mr. MacNeil's 'Liberty' on the new quarter is indeed a beautiful piece of work. The idea conceived by the artist is highly expressive of national sentiment. The figure comes down a flight of steps in an attitude of welcome to the world. In one extended hand she holds a laurel branch of peace, on the left arm she carries a shield. Though she offers peace first she is prepared to defend her honor and her rights. The design suggests a step forward in civilization, protection, and defence, with peace as the ultimate goal.

"In the studio of Mr. MacNeil one has an opportunity of observing some of the intricacies of producing a design for United States currency.

"When Uncle Sam decided he wanted a new quarter he invited three sculptors to submit designs for it. To Mr. MacNeil fell the happy lot of putting his idea into execution.

"Many months of work were necessary before the design was ready to be shown. An idea must be crystallized, and when executing so important a piece of work a sculptor finds it hard to satisfy himself. The first idea does not always seem right. Others are then worked over until a final decision is reached. Then this is done in relief on a medallion 14 inches in diameter. For this work Miss Doscher posed.

"When the first image has been studied, and perhaps changed many times, it is reduced to a medallion five inches in diameter. From this a hard bronze cast is made and sent to the Mint in Philadelphia. From this a reduction is made, this time to the size of the coin, which is just a fraction less than an inch across. This reduction is made through the use of the Janvier machine, and then one is able to see just how the design will look in the size of currency.

"When this is found to be satisfactory a steel model is produced, the steel hardened, and a soft steel mould supplements the die from which come your bright new quarters.

"Making a relief for a coin is very different from making one for any other purpose. There is much to be considered. Especially there must be no crevices in which germs and dirt may collect. Uncle Sam is very particular about this.

"Mr. MacNeil is rightfully delighted in the fact that his work was accepted for the quarter. What sculptor would not be?

"As for the coin girl, her pride is just what you would expect to find in a wholesome, ambitious young woman upon whom this honor had been placed."

With all the effort that went into the coin and the number of people who saw the enlarged version, it is surprising that no one noticed certain "shocking" aspects of the coin. To the horror of many citizens, Miss Liberty appeared on the coin with not only a generous portion of thigh showing under her garment, she also had one bare breast.

The news resulted in a rash of complaints to the government—and probably sent many young boys scurrying out to find the new coins in hopes of a peek at the design that was embarrassing their elders. The nation was in an uproar.

Revelation of the "lewd" aspects of the design proved a great embarrassment to the Government. So many people had seen and approved the original coin that there was no way to place the blame on one individual. As a result, the Government took what many people feel was a typical response—it officially refused to acknowledge the problem. Even MacNeil chose to ignore the rapidly mounting criticism. In one interview with the press he stressed the fact that the coin should not have

The "obscene" Standing Liberty Quarter for 1917.

crevices which attract dirt. However, it was not the physical health of the nation but its morals which was the real issue. But that fact would not come out at the time.

In April, 1917, goaded by moralists, Congress began debating the need for changes in the new quarter. The only official excuse given for going to this expense was that bankers found that the coins "did not stack well." No one was about to mention that the real reason was that Miss Liberty was "stacked" too well.

Senator Warren was skeptical about the stacking information his colleague, Senator Owen, had mentioned. He said, "After the experience we had some years ago with the St. Gaudens coin that would not stack and we had to provide for a new die, I would like to ask the author of the bill how it happens a model is accepted and adopted as the law of the land before it is known whether the coins will stack?"

Senator Owen replied, "It was found after they had actually made them that they did not stack well and for that reason it became of some importance to change the die. I do not know how it occurred in the first place, but they have to change the position of the eagle in order to prevent the coins from toppling when stacked."

On June 25, 1917, a letter from Secretary of the Treasury W. G. McAdoo to Congressman William Ashbrook, Chairman of the Committee on Coinage, Weights and Measures, was read into the Congressional Record. It stated, "I have the honor to submit for your consideration a draft of an act to authorize the modification of the design of the current quarter dollar in accordance with a specimen submitted by Mr. Hermon A. MacNeil, the sculptor whose designs on May 23, 1916 for the quarter dollar now being issued.

"The modifications proposed are slight, and principal one being that the eagle has been raised and three of the stars placed beneath the eagle. On the reverse the lettering has been rearranged and the collision with the pinions of the wings obviated. These changes together with a slight concavity will produce a coin materially improved in artistic merit and not interfere in any way with its practical use.

"I am sorry to have to ask for this change, but since the original dies were made the artist has found that they are not true to the original design and that a great improvement can be made in the artistic value and appearance of the coin by making the slight changes the act contemplates."

Changes in the coin design had already been made. A letter had been sent by MacNeil to Mint Director F. J. Von Engelken in January, 1917, requesting that certain changes be made. Von Engelken replied, in part, "The changes you propose have been read with interest, and it may be practicable to conform to your wishes to some extent. However, as the coins have gone into circulation, no marked changes could be undertaken.

"If you care to have prepared and sent to the Mint a bronze cast carrying the changes you suggest, and will do this with the understanding that the Government is not to be involved in any expense whatever, I will have dies made at the Mint and have specimen coins struck for submission to the Secretary of the Treasury. No radical changes would be considered, and I would reserve the right to decline to execute dies if the model submitted showed a departure from the accepted design."

The changes were made, approved by Secretary McAdoo, and sent to the Committee on Coinage, Weights, and Measures. The final result was a bill which read: "Monetary Legislation (Public No. 27—65th Congress)

"An ACT providing for the modification of the design of the current quarter dollar.

"Be it enacted by the Senate and House of Representatives of the United States of America in Congress assembled, That for the purpose of increasing the artistic merit of the current quarter dollar, the Secretary of the Treasury be, and is hereby, authorized to make slight modifications in the details of the designs in accordance with sketches submitted by the sculptor whose models were accepted under date of May twenty-third, nineteen hundred and sixteen, and now being used in the execution of the coins.

"No changes shall be made in the emblems or devices used. The modifications shall consist of the changing of the position of the eagle, the re-arrangement of the stars and lettering, and a slight concavity given to the surface. Such changes shall be made and completed on or before July first, nineteen hundred and eighteen.

"Approved July 9, 1917."

When the coin design was changed, the eagle had been raised and three stars had been placed below it. The various alterations needed to make a stackable coin were made, but the significant change, and one which was officially never mentioned, was the bringing of modesty to Miss Liberty. On the newly designed coins, her garments had been increased so that her bosom was covered and her thigh was not quite so well revealed.

And so America's only "obscene" coin passed into oblivion. Miss Liberty regained her lost modesty and the nation settled down to the more serious business of fighting World War I.

16

The "Love" Coinage of Edward VIII

Many people talk about the "romance" of coin collecting, but few realize that just a few years ago British coinage was greatly changed because of one of the most dramatic love stories of all times. This is the tale of a monarch who abandoned his throne to follow his heart.

He was born Edward Albert Christian George Andrew Patrick David of the English Royal house of Saxe-Coburg-Gotha. It was the year of 1894 and his home was the royal estate of White Lodge in Richmond Park, Surrey, near London.

Edward was groomed for leadership from the start. He was given private schooling designed to prepare him for the duties of a reigning monarch. On February 18, 1907, he entered the Royal Naval College at Osborne, an action encouraged by his father. His education would be interrupted three years later when his grandfather, King Edward VII, died. George V, young Edward's father, ascended the throne and Edward became the Duke of Cornwall. This title always went to the King's oldest son and provided him with an income of a size to make him financially independent. When he turned 16 he was also named Prince of Wales.

The young Prince was quick to gain the favor of the people. He was confirmed by the Archbishop of Canterbury, Dr. Randall Thomas Davidson, on June 2, 1910. Later he made the traditional speech to the Welsh people, delighting them by being the first British Prince to address them in their native tongue.

Edward entered the military during World War I, attaining the rank of Major. After the war he began traveling as a representative of the monarchy. His journey took him to North America, South America, Africa, the South Pacific, and countless other areas. He was also considered the nation's social leader and was quite active at various public functions.

The women in Edward's life were many, but serious relationships were few. Some of the women were in awe of his position as a member of the royal family. They were either afraid to talk with him or were so taken by his title that they never tried to get to know Edward as a man.

Other women maintained the Victorian attitudes which still dominated England. Under Queen Victoria women had been expected to be secondary to their men. If they dared to have opinions of their own, they were expected to keep them to themselves. Such an attitude seemed foolish to the Prince who longed for someone more challenging than the women he encountered.

Edward's life changed radically in 1931. He had just returned from a trip to South America and joined his brother in Melton Mowbray, Leicestershire, for a weekend of fox hunting. Among the other guests were an American couple, a Mr. and Mrs. Ernest Simpson.

Mrs. Simpson had been born Wallis Warfield, the daughter of a prominent family which had fallen on hard times (her cousin, the writer Upton Sinclair, claimed she was a descendant of the Indian Pocahontas). Wallis' father died while she was still a child, leaving so little money that her mother was forced to take in boarders to make ends meet.

Wallis' education was financed by wealthy relatives who put her through private schools catering to the social elite. She was among the Baltimore debutantes presented at the Bachelor's Cotillion Club, the greatest honor a young society member could achieve.

Wallis was married for the first time in the same year that she made her debut. Her husband was Win Spencer, a pilot with the U.S. Naval Air Service. Together they traveled to China where she left her husband to spend the following year visiting Peking and several other cities. She broadened her knowledge and interests, expanding herself beyond the social orientations of the rather narrow-minded schools in which she had been educated. She also outgrew her husband. They were soon divorced.

Wallis's second marriage was to Ernest Simpson. He was a New Yorker and a Harvard College graduate who had been a member of the Coldstream Guards in World War I. He was so impressed with the British people that he became a naturalized British citizen after the war. He was still married when he began his affair with Wallis, an affair similar to the one she would later have with Edward. They were married in London in 1928 after Simpson's divorce became final.

The weather was miserable when the Simpsons met the Prince for the first time. Wallis had a head cold and was feeling irritable. She was not impressed with royalty, feeling that the entire system was an amusing curiosity that was archaic and a waste of money. She certainly had no respect for a man's title nor was she about to pay homage to someone whose only achievement was having been born the son of a monarch.

Edward approached Wallis the way he did any woman. He started an inane conversation about how she liked living in a country without central heating. This was about the same as his asking a British woman how she liked the weather. He figured she would give an equally meaningless answer so he could smile, nod, and move on to the men who might have something interesting to discuss.

"Every American woman who comes to your country is always asked that same question," she snapped, coldly. "I had hoped for something more original from the Prince of Wales."

Edward was astounded. A woman had never spoken so candidly to him before. He was conceited enough to think that women did not have minds of their own, but Wallis changed that preconceived notion. He later commented:

"A man in my position seldom encountered that trait in other people. Never having believed that my offhand judgements were infallible, I always welcomed a chance to argue them—perhaps because I had so few opportunities of doing so."

As time passed Edward encountered Mrs. Simpson with increasing frequency. He discovered that she enjoyed literature, theater, society, and the world around her. She was a voracious reader of books and magazines and became genuinely interested when new subjects were discussed. Other women just pretended to listen to what the Prince considered intelligent conversation but Wallis was always an active participant.

Wallis became involved in the Prince's public life as well. Most people felt sorry for him for having to participate in what they thought were boring social functions. But Wallis had the attitude that the social functions were obligations he could not change so he might as well make the best of them rather than wallowing in self-pity.

The couple's interest in each other grew with every meeting. At first they were drawn together by mutual curiosity. She was interested in knowing a member of the royal family simply because she had never made such an acquaintance before. He was intrigued by her frankness and intellect. They were cultivating each other's friendship rather than thinking of establishing a romantic relationship.

Soon Edward was inviting the Simpsons to visit him. Wallis often went alone when her husband had to be away on a business trip, and at other times the couple would go together. However, Edward and Ernest Simpson had so little in common that Simpson seemed more like a chaperone for his wife than an invited guest. It became obvious that a romance was blossoming and Wallis was making plans to file for divorce.

By 1935 Edward was thinking seriously about Wallis. He complained to friends that it was unfair for a Prince to be unable to choose any woman he wanted for his bride. The Marriage Act of 1772 was still in force and it placed Royal princes under control of both the Sovereign and Parliament. The King is titular head of the Church of England, a religion that does not recognize divorce. The king's personal life thus had to be a model of propriety. In fact, up through the reign of Edward VII, neither party in a divorce action could be entertained at court no matter whose fault the divorce might have been.

Edward's friends realized how serious he was about Wallis but they also knew that he had been raised for the throne. They were certain he would either break off with Wallis when it was time to take command, or satisfy everyone by making her his mistress. Everyone knew that marriage was out of the question, even after Wallis filed for divorce.

When King George V died, the Prince of Wales became King Edward VIII. It was January 20, 1936, and the new king was 41 years old. Edward at last was able to become involved in work he felt was of importance.

Coin designers and medalists went to work immediately preparing issues to honor the new King. Crowned and uncrowned portraits of Edward had to be produced for the official coinage of Britain and the countries of the Empire. There would also be coronation medals, the Great Seal of the Realm, a series of Government seals and postage stamps.

T. H. Paget, a member of the Royal Mint's art staff, was preparing a likeness of Edward at the time of King George's death. The work had been commissioned privately by the Honourable Company of Master Mariners who were preparing a medal design. The medal would show the Prince on the obverse since one of his titles was Master of the Company.

The Deputy Mint Master knew of Paget's commission and had always liked the artist's work. He asked him to prepare a second model in a low, flat relief that would be suited to coinage. When it was completed, the model was shown to the Royal Mint Advisory Committee which approved the use of the head but not the entire model.

By February the wax likeness of the King had been prepared. It met with the Committee's approval and they decided that additional artistic competition would be unnecessary. They were all set to authorize coinage when the model was sent to the King for formal approval. His reaction was to prove quite surprising.

Britain has always been a nation of traditions. For over 300 years, custom had decreed that coins and stamps would always show a ruler's face looking in the opposite direction of the monarch who had preceded him. King George V had faced left, for example, so it was was assumed that Edward VIII would face right. This was not to be the case, however. The vain Edward had carefully studied his reflection in the mirror and concluded that his left profile was far superior to his right. He would not allow his right profile to be used for the coins.

At first a compromise solution was sought. Why not use the features of his left side but put them in such a way that the head would be facing right? It seemed the perfect answer until Edward vetoed it. The King said that the manner in which he parted his hair on the left side was one of his better points. He would not allow a change if the hair line would be that of the right side of his face.

Coin preparation always takes time so the public was not aware of the behind-the-scenes turmoil the Mint was experiencing at first. However, a hint of what was happening came with the issuance of postage stamps rushed into print at the change of rulers. The stamps followed Edward's wishes. Unfortunately the background originally prepared for the stamps was made to show the King facing right. When the postal authorities learned of his wishes, they changed position of the head but not the background. Thus the King appeared to be looking into the shade rather than into the sun—a bad omen. The London *Times* would comment on the stamps, after the abdication. It said:

"Even the strong minds can yield to this weakness, the superstitious anxiety of those who shook apprehensive heads at the new stamps, because the head of King Edward VIII was turned away from the light, and looked forward into the gloom—apt symbol of a reign that began with everything in its favour and moved onward into calamity."

While the King's vanity was causing postal and money problems, his love life was also of concern. Official pressure was brought by Prime Minister Stanley Baldwin who had regular meetings with him regarding Mrs. Simpson. Edward would later comment: "The Prime Minister trying to help his sovereign through a personal situation of almost indescribable complexity, as that of a political Procrustes determined to fit his regal victim into the iron bed of convention."

Publicly the King and Mrs. Simpson were subject to vicious gossip. Royalty was fascinating to the people, and when a King was interested in a commoner. . . .

The trouble was compounded when Wallis discovered that her husband was being as unfaithful to her as she was to him. She chanced upon a letter he had accidentally misaddressed. It revealed that he was not the silently suffering victim of an errant wife but had taken comfort with another woman. She decided to end the sham of their marriage by publicly filing for divorce. Unfortunately, this only added to the rumors. People thought her actions were taken simply because Edward had become King and could make his own decisions regarding the selection of a wife.

On April 9, 1936, King Edward VIII again defied tradition when he attended the Maundy Thursday Ceremony in Westminister Abbey. He followed custom by donating coins to the poor, but refused to use coins bearing his portrait. He said that he wanted the ceremony to be carried out as though his father was still alive. The special Maundy silver coins would, for 1936 only, bear the portrait of George V. There would be many years ahead for Edward to have his own coinage, or so he reasoned.

Edward did not realize that he had passed up his last chance to appear on the coins of Britain. However, those who received the coins were probably pleased with the decision, though not because they cared whose likeness was on the money. The male and female recipients of the Maundy money were each always equal in number to the age of the monarch whose likeness appeared on the coins. George V would have been 71, so almost 60 more people received coins than would have gotten them had young Edward been portrayed.

In addition to the silver coins, Edward passed out 50 shillings to each of the 71 men and 35 shillings to each of the 71 women. This was provided in place of the gifts of food and clothing that had formerly been presented to the poor.

In mid-April Deputy Mint Master Paget and Percy Metcalfe, an artist commissioned to prepare crowned portraits of the King, visited Edward to discuss the plaster coin models. Edward reiterated his insistence that the uncrowned portrait be facing left rather than facing right with left profile features showing. The way he parted his hair was just too important to be omitted. However, he would allow left profile features to appear in the crowned head portrait so it could be placed looking in either direction. The crown would hide his hairline.

The Deputy Mint Master realized there was no use in argument. Edward was King. If he chose to defy tradition the action might be unpopular, but it could not be appealed.

Paget began work anew, producing a model of the left side of the King's face. A second artist, a sculptor named William McMillan who had previously turned down a commission to produce the reverse for the originally planned coins, was also asked to try his hand at an obverse design. The request came from the President of the Royal Academy who felt a member of that august body should compete for the honor of designing the coin. Since McMillan was a member and Paget was not, McMillan felt obligated to agree to take on the work.

Both artists had made several models by summer. One of Paget's designs and three of McMillan's were made into dies for the striking of trial pieces. Technically, McMillan's coins excelled. However, Paget had worked from life, the King posing for him. McMillan had used only photographs and his portrait was rather stiff and cold. Paget's seemed closer to the King's real personality, so his design was selected for the pattern pieces.

The reverse of the coins was not a problem. There was discussion about changing it but a decision was reached to let well enough alone. The reverse for the silver coins had been in use less than ten years. It was a design by George Kruger Gray which seemed useable with only slight modification. The halfcrown and florin coin designs had a "G" incorporated as a tribute to the late King George. If that was removed, the reverse would be perfect for Edward's coinage.

Once again no one had reckoned with the personal taste of the King. He became angry when informed of the decision of the Advisory Committed of the Royal Mint to keep the old reverse. He wanted a coinage that was uniquely his own. The reverse should be new and in a modern style rather than imitating the type of reverse which had traditionally appeared on the coins over the years.

The King was not articulate about his definition of a "modern" reverse. The Deputy Mint Master and his staff of artists felt that the King would not be happy with such radical approaches as cubism. They also felt that heraldry could be continued on the coins if it was handled in a new and different manner. They even thought of using animals, birds, or plants in the design but since there was nothing unique to Britain that they could select they decided to drop that concept.

Another design consideration also had to be made. The Royal Style and Titles always appeared on the obverse of coins, with a portion spilling over to the reverse due to lack of space. Past reverses had been made to incorporate this Latin writing into the heraldry. They wondered if a radically new approach could still contain the writing.

Wilson Parker was the first artist to devise a new design. His sketches, revealed in May, showed reverses based on the Crown and objects relating to the life of Britain and her Empire. The coins utilized swans, wrens, eagles, doves, deer, and other creatures.

Kruger Gray, another artist, produced more traditional reverses for his offerings. These used variations of the Heraldry concept.

When the possible reverse designs were shown to the King, he was delighted by Parker's concepts. Unfortunately he realized that the gossip about his love affair had become so extensive that it would not be wise to add to the wrath of the people by ordering radically different coinage. He made the final selection from the Kruger designs which were not such a break from tradition.

Oddly, the Deputy Mint Master either misunderstood the reasons behind the King's selection or wanted to come up with an excuse for the rejection which would be easier for Parker to take. He told the artist that the type of animals he used had been the reason his designs were not used. He pointed out that the eagle was an American symbol which had also appeared on the coins of Italy and Germany, countries against which there were hard feelings. The dove was a passive bird, not at all the proper symbol for a nation facing war. And the rendering of the swan looked more like a goose. He eased his criticism by adding that if other animals had been used, his designs might have been accepted.

Parker's designs were accepted for the bronze coinage. The wren concept, rejected for the silver coins, was adopted for the Farthing. The figure of Britannia, traditional on coins since the 1600s, was modified from previous concepts but retained on the bronze penny. The half-crown and half-penny reverses were variations on designs Paget had developed when he was trying to find a new reverse for the silver coins.

The only coin that ever went into circulation was the nickel-brass threepence. Its entry into circulation was accidental, however.

The threepence was a radical design change. It was 12-sided and combined the Paget version of the uncrowned head of Edward with a reverse designed by Miss Frances Madge Kitchener, the niece of a member of the House of Lords. Trial pieces were struck to see how the coins would fit into existing slot machines. The coins were taken to the machine manufacturers who experimented with them and were then supposed to return them to the Mint. Up to a dozen of them managed to get into circulation, however, turning up occasionally in change.

The tests indicated that the coins had to be thicker and Percy Metcalfe altered the Kitchener design to facilitate striking. Pattern pieces of the modified coin were produced the early part of December.

Gold coinage proved the least troublesome. Britain went off the gold standard in 1931 so the only gold pieces to be struck were for use in Proof sets. These were not regular issues so Edward had little interest in their design. It was decided that since Pistrucci's St. George and the Dragon, which was first used on sovereigns in 1817, had been used continuously on gold since 1893, the tradition might as well continue.

While Edward was arguing about coinage, Wallis was arguing about her life with her husband. The Simpsons' divorce case reached court on October 27. Edward was careful to ignore the event though stories did appear in the newspapers. In deference to the King, the reports of the proceedings were restrained and no mention was made of Edward's involvement.

By mid-November Edward was determined to make Mrs. Simpson his wife, a decision which outraged his family. His mother, Queen Mary, felt, "One divorce could seldom or never be justified, and to divorce twice, on any grounds whatsoever, was," to her, "unthinkable," according to her biographer, Pope-Hennessy.

The Queen's background was rather interesting. She had accepted an arranged marriage with a man who had died before the wedding day. She then willingly married the man's brother, who later became King George V. She firmly believed that personal feelings should always be sacrificed for the greater good of the country. She felt that Edward had never sacrificed himself in war so the least he could do was subvert his feelings towards Mrs. Simpson.

The family made several suggestions as to how Edward could handle his relation. Recognizing the depth of his feelings, they said he might want to make Wallis Simpson his mistress. She could be his wife in every way except legally. This was an action many kings had taken in the past. Edward would have nothing to do with such a plan, however. He would not live in sin with the woman he wished to share his name.

An alternative was for the King to have what was known as a morganatic marriage. Such a marriage would result in neither Mrs. Simpson nor her heirs having any titles or claims to royalty. Wallis would be his wife but never a Queen, the title traditionally reserved for whomever married a King.

Morganatic marriages were not new. The Duke of Cambridge, grandchild of King George III, had fallen in love with the actress Louisa Fairbrother. As a result of the Royal Marriage Act of 1772, he had to go to the Queen to seek permission to marry Louisa. The Queen refused so the Duke began living with his beloved. They had two sons before their marriage, without permission, in 1847.

The marriage proved to be a happy one, lasting until Louisa's death 43 years later. Queen Victoria never tried to punish the Duke and his sons had successful careers. However, had he taken the throne, his wife would not have been Queen and his sons would not have been eligible to succeed him.

King George IV had a bigamous morganatic marriage. He was officially married to the Princess Caroline, a woman he detested. He also married Mrs. Fitzherbert, whom he loved, but who could never bear the title of Queen.

Wallis was interested in her husband's future and said she would agree to a morganatic marriage. He felt the idea had been debased over the years and would not subject her to what he thought was humiliation. He knew the people would scorn her and he could not stand for this.

On December 10, 1936, Prime Minister Stanley Baldwin entered the House of Commons to read a message from the King. It stated: "After long and anxious consideration I have become determined to renounce the throne to which I succeeded on the death of my father, and I am communicating this, my final and irrevocable decision. Realising as I do the gravity of this step, I can only hope that I shall have the understanding of my people in the decision I have taken and the reason which have led me to take it. I will not now enter into my private feelings, but I would beg that it should be remembered that the burden which constantly rests upon the shoulders of a sovereign is so heavy that it can only be borne in circumstances different from those in which I now find myself."

The decision had not been an easy one. He knew that his family was against the action and that the newspapers were hostile to the entire affair. However, he was determined to marry Mrs. Simpson and had been warned that such an action would trigger the resignation of the Prime Minister and other government leaders. He felt that a King should unite his country, not divide it. He decided to turn leadership over to his brother, the Duke of York.

A formal statement of abdication was drawn up and signed.

The government leaders were irate over the resignation. They felt that Edward had been disloyal to the nation by not accepting the office that had been his rightful inheritance. Despite the fact that a year's work had gone into coinage design, it was felt that there would be no numismatic honors for the ex-King. Specimen sets were prohibited and all dies had to be defaced or destroyed.

Pattern pieces had been prepared but no official coinage existed for Edward. The British people were thus spared the knowledge of how Edward had planned to break with tradition in the matter of coin design.

When George VI ascended the throne, he had his portrait facing left, supposedly the reverse of what the previous monarch's coinage would have been. Thus many people thought that Edward's only break had been in regard to the postage stamp design.

And so the coinage of Edward VIII came to an end. On December 12, 1936, at 2 A.M., he boarded the British destroyer "Fury" and left England for Boulogne, France. Almost six months later, on June 3, 1937, he married Wallis Simpson and they became the Duke and Duchess of Windsor. Later, during World War II, Edward also became Governor of the Bahama Islands. He died in May, 1972, leaving behind a legacy of coinage limited because of his love for the woman who caused him to abandon his throne.

17

All That Glitters . . .

No story of coins is complete without a brief look at some of the pieces issued through private enterprise. Counterfeit coinage, although a serious problem for both Mint officials and collectors, still has its lighter side. We may curse such spurious issues but we can still be amused by some of the people who have produced them.

Take the case of Charles Butler, for example. Butler was an employee of the San Francisco branch of the United States Mint. For 23 years he worked as a night janitor keeping the work area clean and sparkling. Then in April, 1917, he was suddenly placed under arrest by law enforcement officers who had been hiding in the building when he came on duty.

Butler's criminal activity was the result of his being a loyal and loving husband. Every payday he faithfully turned his pay envelope over to his wife who would then budget the family finances. Unfortunately there was never any extra "walking around" money for Charles who would have enjoyed having an occasional drink with the boys before he came home from work. To solve his problems, Butler used to go into the press room, put a little silver into the mold and make himself a new half dollar. He was never greedy and seldom made more than one or two coins. He just wanted enough so he could afford a little fun before going home.

The janitor's downfall came because he was not really familiar with the operation of the newer equipment. The day shift found that the machines were not in proper working order, the apparent result of an untrained person having used them. A secret, 24-hour stakeout was begun which led to Butler's arrest. How many Butler-made Barber and Walking Liberty Half Dollars are in existence is impossible to say, but there is a chance you have at least one in your collection.

Then there was the case of the Ohio man arrested in the 1950's. He had wife problems too, but in a different way. He had a basement workshop where he would happily spend hour after hour puttering with equipment his wife never had any interest in seeing. He never brought his handiwork up to show her and she never attempted to enter his "lair." As long as he was happy, she was happy.

It was on a sunny afternoon that our story began. The man's wife decided to do a little shopping but discovered that she was short of cash. She called to her husband in his workshop, asking him if he could spare a few dollars. She was answered with silence.

The wife went down to the basement, trying to find him. She knocked on the door of his work room but he failed to respond, so she carefully opened the door and peeked inside. Her husband was not there but he had apparently been thoughtful enough to anticipate her needs. On a table was a stack of Franklin Half Dollars. She took a handful and happily did her shopping.

The clerk in the store knew the woman and did not hesitate to accept her money. But he was suspicious of it. It seemed silly, but the coins looked a little too good to him. They appeared somehow better struck than usual. He felt foolish about his anxiety, yet he decided to turn the coins over to the Secret Service for examination.

It turned out that the coins were counterfeit, made by the woman's husband in his basement workshop. However, rather than being cheap imitations, they were better designed, better engraved, and had more silver than the official government issues. The silver content alone was worth 55 cents at the time!

The man explained that making the coins was his hobby. He never had any intention of passing them and his wife's actions had been the result of a misunderstanding. The court appreciated his dilemma but sentenced him to jail.

Probably the most colorful of all counterfeiters were William Kendig and William Jacobs, two thoroughly larcenous souls. Their first joint crime was the counterfeiting of cigar tax stamps since they were both involved with the manufacture of cigars. (Jacobs had made more money defrauding insurance companies than from his legitimate operations, however.) Cigar manufacturers had to pay a tax on each box of cigars they produced and the stamp was obtained from the government as proof of payment. By counterfeiting the stamps and putting the fakes on a large percentage of the cigars they produced, they were able to greatly increase their profits.

But the counterfeit stamps only served as an exercise in basic larceny. The two men developed a business of much greater interest to numismatists. They decided to produce counterfeit $100 bills.

It was the last half of the 1890's and the nation was still trying to recover from the effects of the recent depression. It was not hard to find two engravers who needed money and did not care how they made it. Baldwin Bredell and Arthur Taylor, previously hired to make the counterfeit tax stamps, were enlisted in the new project—to make 10 million dollars in $100 bills.

The plan was brilliant. The men would open 50 checking accounts in as many different banks throughout the country. Jacobs and Kendig had long been creating various fake companies to serve as fronts for their enterprises and these companies would act as credit references. The money would be left in the accounts for several weeks, then withdrawn and deposited in one bank in either Philadelphia or New York City. The funds would be invested in prime securities and the securities would be split among the four men.

Jacobs, the most successful of the men in his past endeavors, co-ordinated the project, opened the bank accounts, and put up enough of his own money to cover any bribes which might have to be offered to suspicious officials. He would also handle all financing. For this he would receive half the money produced.

Taylor's job was to obtain the printing plates and Bredell was to secure the necessary machinery. Both Bredell and Kendig would try to locate the necessary paper for printing.

Bredell custom designed the printing machinery he would need after going with Kendig to Dalton, Massachusetts. In Dalton, the Crane Company paper mill produced the special paper used for the Government's official currency. The two men had been treated to a tour of the plant which provided them with a good idea of how the paper was made and the silk threads added to the material.

The press was ordered from a Maryland company. It was quite similar to the type used by the Bureau of Printing and Engraving but the order did not arouse any suspicions.

The downfall of most counterfeiters of paper money came because they were not skilled enough to hand engrave an exact duplicate of the bill they wanted to print. However, the new method of photo-engraving had been introduced and Taylor was aware that it was the answer to a counterfeiter's dream. He bought camera equipment capable of photographing the paper money. If a little retouching had to be done later, the retouching would offer fewer risks than producing the entire plate.

Kendig concluded that it would be impossible to obtain the paper they needed. Using the dummy companies again, he ordered tanks and other equipment for making his own paper, setting it up in a warehouse he owned. He also ordered hundreds of pounds of silk threads for adding to the paper.

All the preparations for a successful counterfeiting operation take time and both Taylor and Bredell were not prepared to wait. They were anxious to go into production and felt that the delays were inexcusable. They worked with a regular dollar bill until they learned how to slit it in half, bleach it, insert silk threads, and rice paste it back together. That difficult task accomplished, it was child's play to use their printing plates to produce $100 bills.

Unknown to the partners, Bredell and Taylor produced 97 of the bills and, by mid-July, 1897, they had passed them in areas ranging from Philadelphia to Florida. When their spending spree was over, they placed $8,000 in the bank and Bredell bought his wife a diamond ring. The unmarried Taylor chose, as his last purchase, a new fur coat for his mother. It seems that there is always a little good in every bad boy.

It was not until December that one of the counterfeit bills was first detected. The man who spotted the fake was a teller in the Philadelphia U.S. Sub-Treasury. He was handling a $100 bill which looked and felt perfectly normal except for the seal: it was supposed to be a rich carmine color but the bill he held had a weak pink. Perhaps the machine producing it had not been properly inked, he thought, as did his coworkers to whom he showed the bill.

Alerted by the first $100 bill, the tellers at the Sub-Treasury began examining every bill of that denomination which came to them. Four more notes were found with the same off-color seal.

The five bills were taken by one of the tellers to Washington where they were shown to Treasury officials. Secret Service Agent William Moran, the nation's leading expert on counterfeiting, was also on hand. He stated that the paper was genuine but much too thick. He took one of the bills and placed it in a pan of hot water. Within minutes the two halves separated.

Moran began an intense section-by-section study of the bills. He found that the money was a fraction of an inch too wide and that retouched numbers differed very slightly from those on the real bill. There were several other differences, but it took the nation's leading expert to detect them. The average bank teller, no matter how well trained and alert, would probably be deceived. The public would certainly be fooled.

When the Secretary of the Treasury learned the quality of the fakes, he made an unprecedented decision. The *New York Times* released the story to the public. The article stated, in part: "In view of the dangerous character of the counterfeit, Secretary Gage today decided to stop issuing and to call in all one-hundred-dollar silver certificates of which there are about twenty-six million dollars outstanding. These will be exchanged for silver certificates of smaller denominations and the plates destroyed. As soon as new plates can be engraved, a new series will be issued. Assistant Treasurers at all Sub-Treasury cities will be required to send to the Treasury, in Washington, all one-hundred-dollar silver certificates in their possession and to request all banks, trust companies, and other financial institutions to do the same."

William Jacobs was shocked when he read the newspaper. He knew what must have happened and lashed into Taylor and Bredell with a verbal tirade. He told them they were fools and demanded they turn over the worthless plates.

When Jacobs calmed down enough to discuss the matter with Kendig, the other wronged partner, they decided that the incident showed their faith in the two engravers' abilities had been justified. The plates had been almost perfect. Rather than breaking off ties with the men, they decided to try again, this time watching the engravers' every move. In addition, they would produce bills in several denominations so that a complete recall would be impossible.

Secret Service agents, acting on the assumption that the bills had been made in Philadelphia, journeyed there to search for the counterfeiters. Assuming that the engravers were local men, they made a list of every engraver in the city, checking each one out in arduous, painstaking police work.

Bredell and Taylor's recent, sudden affluence had been noticed by friends and merchants, and it was only a matter of time before the agents were on their trail. Arrests were made and the men were jailed.

But the case did not really come to an end. John Semple, the attorney for Taylor, visited him in prison and commented on previous cases involving skilled counterfeiters. It might be possible, he told his client, to trade the hidden counterfeit plates for a reduction in the prison sentence.

Although Taylor thought the idea an excellent one, he also knew that the only plates he had made at the time of his imprisonment were already in the hands of Secret Service agents. If he and Bredell were going to gain an early release, they would have to manufacture new plates—in prison!

Turn-of-the-century prisons were somewhat different from today's facilities. Taylor and Bredell shared a 9 x 6 x 9 foot cell in Philadelphia's Moyamensing Prison. All their work would have to be accomplished there, a task which proved less difficult than one might think.

Visitors to the prison were never searched, so Taylor's brother, Harry, was able to sneak three steel plates, engraving tools, and a magnifying glass to the men. Only a lawyer could meet directly with the men. Other visitors had to stand outside the cell door. However, all the necessary equipment was easily passed through a slot which was used for passing food and dishes. If the cell was searched at a later time, the men could just hide the items on their persons. The guards were not very sophisticated by today's standards and seldom searched both a cell and its occupants at the same time.

The engraving was handled at night. While one man slept, the other worked under a blanket, using the light from an alcohol lamp to see. A little smuggled nitric acid, and some table salt, the silver from a coin, and some kitchen gelatin were somehow combined to produce a photographic emulsion enabling them to photograph both sides of a real bill. The actual process used has never been released by the Secret Service nor duplicated by others. The photographs were made by slitting a $20 bill and oiling it to make it transparent. It was then placed against the emulsion coated plate and exposed to light. This is something like the paper negative with which some photographers have experimented.

The way they handled the etching was revealed in the memoirs of Secret Service Agent Donald Wilkie. He said, in part: "Examining the genuine note through a glass they found that across its face ran parallel lines, a thousand to the inch, which were invisible to the naked eye . . . With a jeweler's glass, a parallel rule, and a single engraving tool, (Bredell) drew those lines on a sheet of mica of the proper size, rubbed in red paint and polished off the surface with the palm of his hand, calk-

covered, precisely as the Government engravers in Washington polish the ink from their plates. Next he placed the mica, upside down, on the steel plate and set it over his burning candle. (Actually the alcohol lamp—T.S.) The heat cooked the oil paint out of the crevices in the mica and onto the plate where it ate its way into the steel . . . the delicate lines were neatly etched."

Taylor's brother smuggled in 150 one dollar bills which the ingenious prisoners managed to bleach with chemicals concocted from their meals. The currency was soon ready for printing.

Bredell next sent his father the drawings for a new invention—a "cuff ironer." He told the elderly man that he wanted a model made which he could perfect and patent. When the model was smuggled in to him, it turned out to be a highly efficient miniature printing press. With smuggled ink the bleached bills were turned into counterfeit twenties. Then all materials and the finished bills were smuggled out of the prison as easily as they had been brought in.

Harry Taylor managed to circulate 32 of the twenties before one was discovered. The merchant who was involved in the discovery made Harry give him a good bill in its place, which he did. The frightened Harry then returned home and burned the bills. The plates remained buried near his father's grave.

The story did not come to an end. The Secret Service learned of the bogus bill, traced it to Harry and gained a confession. At first everyone claimed that the money was made before the two engravers went to jail. Unfortunately the serial number of the $20 bill they used was one which had been started after the men were sent to prison.

In the end a bargain was made. The engravers told where the plates were hidden and testified against the attorney whose suggestion had led to the plot. In return, Harry Taylor would receive a light sentence and the court would also go easy on the engravers.

When the story finally ended, everyone involved in the counterfeiting operation which had occurred both in and out of prison had to serve sentences. The lone exception was the attorney whose previously spotless record seemed to make an impression on the jury. Although he was twice brought to trial, he was never convicted.

During the first half of the 1800s a less creative but equally enterprising pair of counterfeiters operated out of Kentucky. Jacob and Nancy Sprinkle lived in two small log cabins spaced seven yards apart and joined by an underground tunnel. Their home was on the Kinniconick

River, five miles southeast of the community of Vanceburg. It was an exceptionally rural area and it suffered from a coin shortage.

The United States Mint had only been in operation for a relatively short time and it had not yet begun to produce adequate coinage for circulation throughout the country. Even big cities had coin shortages, but rural developments seldom, if ever, saw official Mint issues. They generally had to rely on a form of barter combined with the use of whatever foreign coins were available. The Sprinkles, being civic-minded, decided to do something for their community. They used the underground passage between their cabins to start their own mint.

The Sprinkles knew of a small, secret silver lode which they could use for the manufacture of their coins. Rather than actually counterfeiting existing pieces, they made unique specie. An owl was on the obverse and a six-pointed star was on the reverse. They were larger than similar government denominations and of greater intrinsic value. They were designed to pass for dollars and were so well made that area merchants would refuse a U.S. dollar if a Sprinkle dollar was available instead.

Time passed and the Kentucky community began to grow. A county prosecutor, probably anxious about re-election, decided that it was time to end the Sprinkles' lawlessness. He brought them to court, but his case was lost before he could start. The judge, Walker Reed, pulled out a handful of Sprinkle dollars and told the jury, "I defy the United States to produce from their mints dollars as good as these I hold in my hand." Since the prosecutor had not even begun to present his case at that point, it was obvious that the jury had been prejudiced from the start.

When the jury deadlocked, a new trial was ordered. No one wanted them to go through this ordeal, however, so the Sprinkles abandoned their mint and moved to California where they conveniently "died." At least that is what their attorney said when he introduced their faked death certificates when their second trial was scheduled to begin. "You can't prosecute dead people," the judge announced, officially ending the case.

There was another counterfeiter who delighted his community with actions which made his name into a common American expression. This was Josh Tatum, a deaf mute who had the good fortune to be living back in 1883 when the Liberty Head Nickel was introduced into circulation. The coin, with the head of Liberty on the obverse and a v on the reverse, seemed quite similar to a $5 gold piece to many people. The gold coin did have a Liberty Head, although of different design. The rest

The 1883 Liberty Head Nickel without the word CENTS. This coin was gold plated and passed as a $5 gold piece.

Reverse of the 1883 Liberty Head Nickel.

The altered reverse of the Liberty Head Nickel with the word CENTS added.

of the coin was so dissimilar that it is amazing that so many people could have been fooled. However, when the coin was painted gold many businessmen accepted it as a $5 gold piece, as Josh Tatum discovered.

Tatum was not the only man passing the gold plated nickels as genuine gold pieces, but he was both the most clever and the most successful. Tatum was quite selective about his victims. His habit was to walk into a cigar store, point to a nickel cigar, and lay one of the gold plated coins on the counter. If the clerk had the sense to recognize the coin as a five cent piece, Tatum would simply walk out with his paid-in-full purchase. However, most of the time the clerk would hand Tatum $4.95 in change which he graciously accepted.

Tatum's deceptions brought him wealth, fame, and his day in court. At the trial his defense attorney stated that Tatum was deaf and "dumb." He explained that Tatum had not tried to deceive anyone, for all his purchases never exceeded five cents. He added that since Tatum was unable to speak, it was impossible for him to argue with a clerk who chanced to give him too much money.

The judge was angered by Tatum's actions and gave him a warning that he must never spend gold plated nickels again. However, it was impossible to prove that a law had been broken and Tatum was released.

The final result was both the adding of the word "cents" to later issues (both Tatum and others passed an estimated 10,000 gold plated nickels) and the introduction of a new word to the English language. By 1895 everyone in the United States knew that to "josh" or "I was just joshing" meant to joke or tease. Tatum's name became a part of the nation's vocabulary.

Our last story is not really about a counterfeiter but about a dishonest engraver who was a frequent prison inmate between the years 1850 and 1875. In order to keep his artist's skills while incarcerated, he developed the hobby of changing the rather regal looking Seated Liberty Half Dollar into something akin to pornography.

With the engraving tools the guards allowed him to have, the inmate carefully removed Liberty's clothing. Then he filled out the body so she became a naked voluptuous figure. He also re-engraved her shield so, when he was finished, it appeared that she was seated on a chamber pail.

Notes on the Chapters

Chapters 2 and 3

The coins of the Roman Empire could be broken down according to the following system:

One gold Aureus was equal to 25 silver denarii.

One silver Denarius was equal to four bronze sestertii.

One silver Quinarius was equal to two bronze sestertii.

One orichalcum (yellow bronze alloy of copper and zinc)
Sestertius was equal to four copper asses.

One orichalcum Dupondius was equal to two copper asses.

One copper As was equal to four quadrantes.

In contrast, during the earliest days of Rome coins were valued by weight, resulting in the following system:

One As equaled one pound (based on 12 ounces to the pound) and was valued 1.

One Semis equaled one-half pound and had a value mark of S.

One Tremis equaled four ounces as was marked • • • •

One Quadrans equaled three ounces and was marked • • •

One Sextans equaled two ounces and was marked • •

One Unica equaled one ounce and was marked •

Chapter 4

The esteem in which John Hull was held may be seen by reading of the sermon delivered at his funeral by Samuel Willard. It is taken from *The High Esteen Which God Hath Of The Death Of His Saints,* published in Boston in 1683. It reads:

"1. When the Saints die let us mourn: And there is no greater Argument to be found that we should excite our selves to mourn by, then the remembrance that they were Saints: it should more effect our hearts at the thoughts of this that they were Saints, then that they were our Father, or Mother, or Brethren, or nearest or dearest Friends, for this is that which makes their loss to be greater than any other Relation doth or can; others are natural, but these are pious Tears that are shed upon this account: Another Man may be a private loss when he is gone, his Family or his Neighbours, or Consorts may miss him; but a Saint, though he be a private Christian, is yet, when he dies, a publick loss, and deserves the tears of Israel; how much more than when he hath been a Saint providentially put into a capacity of being, and by Grace helpt and enabled to be a publick benefit by the Orb he moved in? when a Saint Dies there is manifold ground of Mourning; there is then a Pillar pluckt out of the Building, a Foundation Stone taken out of the Wall, a Man removed out of the Gap; and now it is to be greatly feared that God is departing and Calamities are coming and are not these things to be lamented?

"2. When the Saints die beware of irregular Mourning: though we are to lament their Death, yet we much beware that it be after the right manner: a dying Saint may say to his weeping Friends that stand round about, wringing their hands, after the same Language that Christ did to those weeping Women, Luk. 23, 27, 28, 29. Daughters of Jerusalem, weep not for me, but for your selves, and your Children, &c. It is we and not they that are indangered and endamaged by it: we may therefore weep for our selves, and there is good reason for it, but to mourn for them is superfluous. Is the Death precious in Gods? let it not be miserable in our esteem: and tell me you whose hearts throb, and eyes run over with sorrow, it is not a precious thing to be asleep in Jesus? to ly in the lap of his providence, and rest from the labours and sorrows of a troublesome World? to be laid out of the noise of the whistling Winds, and feel none of the impetuosity of those Storms and Tempests that are blowing abroad? to be laid out of the sight and hearing of the rolling and dashing waves of the roaring Sea? to sleep out the rest of the tempestuous night of this world, standing in the inner Chamber of Gods Providence, in answer to that sweet invitation? Isai. 26.22. Come my People, enter into thy Chambers and shut thy doors about thee, &c . . .

"3. Is the death of the Saints precious in God's sight? Let it be so in ours, too. They are not to be accounted for contemptible things which God sets an high value upon; and it is our wisdom to think and speak of persons and things as God doth: we ought not to slight the death of the righteous, and speak meanly of it, as of a thing that is little momentous: I am sure their arrival at Heaven is there taken notice of as a thing worthy of observation; and shall not their departure be regarded? they are welcomed into the Palace of delight with Panegyricks; and shall then be hence dismissed with no more but a sorry saying, there is now a good man gone, and he will be missed in the Family, or the Church to which he once belonged? we should embalm the memory of the Saints with the sweet smelling Spices that grew in their own Gardens, and pick the chiefest Flowers out of those Beds to strew their Graves withal; we should remember and make mention of them with honourable thoughts and words: and though it be now grown a Nickname of contempt amoung wicked and prophane Men, yet count it the most orient Jewel in their Crown, the most odoriferous and pleasant Flower in their Garland, that we can say of them that they lived and died Saints; all other Escutcheons will either wear away, or be taken down, every other monument will become old, and grow over with the Moss of time, and their Titles, though cut in Brass, will be Canker-eaten and illegible: this only will endure and be fresh and flourishing, when Marble itself shall be turned into common dust.

"Such an one it is whom we have now lost and Oh that we knew how great a loss we have sustained in him! they are little things to be put into the account, and weigh but light in the commendations we have to give him; to say, This Government hath lost a Magistrate; this Town hath lost a good Benefactor; this Church hath lost an honourable Member; his Company hath lost a worthy Captain; his Family hath lost a loving and kind Husband, Father, Master; the Poor have lost a Liberal and Merciful Friend; that nature had furnished him with a sweet and affable Disposition, and even temper; that Providence had given him a prosperous and Flourishing Portion of this Worlds Goods; that the love and respect of the People had lifted him up to places of honour and preferment; this, this outshines them all; that he was a Saint upon Earth, and now is gone to rest with the Saints in glory: this hath raised those Relicks of his above common dust, and made them precious dust. When Conscience of duty stimulated me to perform my part of his Exequies, and put me upon it to do him honour at his Death; methoughts Justice required, and envy itself would not nibble at this Character: and if the Tree be to be known by its Fruits, his works shall praise him in the Gates: For his constant and close secret Communion with God (which none but Hypocrites are wont to do with the sound of a Trumpet) such are were most intimate with him, have known and can testifie: the care which he had to keep up constant Family Worship, in reading of the Scriptures, and praying in his Family (from which no business publick or private could divert him) was almost now unparalled; the honourable respect he bore to God's holy Ordinances, by diligently attending upon them, and esteeming highly of God's Servants for their work sake, and care that he used to live the Truths which he heard from time to time, was very singular: the exemplariness of his Life and Converse amoung Men, and the endeavours which he used to shew forth the Graces of the Spirit, not being ashamed of Christ, nor being willing to be a shame unto him; let all that knew him bear witness of: his meek boldness in reproving Sin, and gentle faithfulness in endeavouring to win Sinners as he had opportunity, is known to such as lay in his way: His constancy in all these whiles times have changed, and many professors have degenerated, when he strove to grow better as the times grew worse, will speak the sincerity of his Profession: his living above the World, and keeping his heart disentangled, and his mind in Heaven, in the midst of all outward occasions and urgency of Business, bespake him not to be of this World, but a Pilgrim on the Earth, a Citizen of Heaven: In a word, he was a true Nathaniel.

"But God hath taken him from us, and by this stroak given us one more sad prognostick of misery a coming: when there are but a few Saints in the World, and those die apace too, what is to be thought to be at the door? I dare say his Death was precious in God's sight, and he had the same holy end in taking him away just now, who might probably have lived many years, and done much more service for God in his Generation: I shall not make it my work to Prophesie; the Lord grant we do not all know it too soon to our cost. Mean time let us have such in remembrance, and labour to be followers of them who through Faith and Patience do not inherit the primises, and that will be the best way to divert the Omen: Let us account the Saints precious whiles they live, and God will not begrutch them to us: but if we by contempt, obloquy, and wickedly grieving their Righteous Souls, make their lives a burden to them, if they cannot live in honour amoung Men, they shall die in favour with God, and he will make their death a precious gain to them, though coming upon those whom they leave behind them."

Chapter 5

Coins other than large cents have had unusual uses. One of the most interesting and certainly the sexiest happened in the Near East. Belly dancers entertaining the public received tips from their appreciative audiences. The coins given in this fashion were carefully attached to the dancer's costume until her entire body was decorated with silver and gold. These coins became the girl's dowry, enabling her to "purchase" a husband. She had to make her money while she could, however. Once she married her public dancing days were over and she could only perform for the enjoyment of her husband.

According to the back-to-nature buff, a silver coin was once considered invaluable for telling the difference between good and bad mushrooms growing in the wild. A coin and the gathered mushrooms were dropped into a frying pan. If the mushrooms were bad, the coin would turn black. How accurate this test might have been is not known. It certainly is not a practice to copy because if it does not work the result could be a severe poisoning!

Coins were placed around children's necks during colonial times to ward off witches and evil spirits.

Coins are often thought to be lucky pieces which, when placed in a new wallet, insure that the owner will never be broke. Good fortune is also believed to follow the person who throws a coin in a fountain.

At least one doctor used a quarter as part of a bandage, taping the coin over the umbilical hernia of an infant. The tape was replaced at regular intervals until the hernia was reduced.

The Irish once believed that a coin had to be included when giving a friend a knife or other sharp implement as a present; otherwise the relationship would be severed.

A silver sixpence placed in a British bride's shoe insured a lifetime of good fortune and happiness.

Trade dollars were made into heavy skirts in the Far East. And in Sarawak the dead were buried in clothing made out of silver coins that had been dyed purple.

Columnist Mort Reed reports that coins have been used as weapons of war. Chalabi Rumi Khan, a Mohammedan, ran out of ammunition during a war with the Hindus. He fired cannons filled with bags of coins, defeating his enemy.

1/10d pieces served as washers on roofs in British West Africa. A large headed nail was placed through the coin hole to hold the roofing material in place.

Everyone knows about the Tooth Fairy's gifts of coins. Whenever a child loses a tooth, anything from a dime to a half dollar is liable to turn up under the child's pillow.

Finally comes a story from Robert Clarke, a geologist working in Iran. He wrote me of his early days scouting exploratory wells being drilled in West Texas and Southeastern New Mexico. He said, "In this area most waters associated with the Permian dolomite productive zones were salt saturated and the main water zone beneath the production was sulfur bearing as well. Thus it was extremely important to know if water being bailed from cable tool wells was sulfur bearing or only salty. Many wells in those days were not drilled with rotary tools and mud as is the case today. Water samples were obtained by bailing.

"The experienced geologists taught me how to dip a bright silver coin in the water to be tested. If the coin turned black the failure of the well was apparent—if it remained shiny the drilling would continue.

"After each use the quarter had to be cleaned with soda in preparation for the next water test," Clarke continues. "I carried the same quarter in my pocket until my geologic career was interrupted by World War II. After the war my duties no longer called for this type of activity and one day I learned that my 'black' quarter (1932-S) had become valuable. Now the quarter is retired and rests in an honored spot in my collection—still black for old times' sake."

Chapter 10

On July 1, 1866, new rules and regulations regarding the special striking of coins, the disposition of patterns and the selling of specimens from the Mint holding went into effect. It read, in part:

". . . To aid in the execution of Medal and Coin dies, the Mint nearly thirty years ago, imported the French Machine, the Tour a' Portrait of Contamine, for making dies from models. The Mint has recently contracted for, and is daily expecting, Hill's Engraving Machine, purchased under authority of Hon. Hugh McCulloch, Secretary of the Treasury, an English invention, for which it is claimed that for its superior powers, and singular ingenuity, it will supersede the other apparatus. We therefore expect to do justice to any orders, at a less expense, and in less time, than under the former system.

"The occasion calls for a revision of our operations in this line, and for some reduction of prices, as will be found in the annexed schedule. And as cognate branches, it is proposed to unite therewith, the annual issue of proof or master coins of the regular series, as heretofore; and the specimen or 'pattern' coins which are not adopted, or do not become so, within the year of their date. (The term 'pattern' is used here, out of deference to the technicalities of collectors, not because of its peculiar fitness; for if the piece fails to be adopted, it is not properly a pattern. 'Experimental' is a better term.) These last have hitherto been given out, or withheld by no rule whatsoever; although they have by degrees attained to a very considerable importance, on account of the eagerness of many collectors to obtain them. There is, indeed, a pretty strong reason, why these should be used only for their special purpose; namely to aid the Treasury Department, or a Congressional Committee, in forming an idea of the size, appearance and practicability of any newly proposed coin, or of any change of devices in an old one. But it has been found impossible to put this rigid limit upon them. If we strike only a few, the ambitious collector will have one at any price; and a competition IS CREATED, OUT OF ALL PROPORTIONS TO THE MERITS OF THE PRIZE. It seems better, therefore, avoiding the error of making such pieces too plentiful, to give some scope to the acquisition of them.

"This whole department will be under the supervision of the DIRECTOR OF THE MINT, and all inquiries and requests, with or without money, must be addressed to him. The medals and coins will be in the responsible custody of one of his clerks, who will also attend to the orders, reply to letters, and keep the accounts. The making of dies and the striking of medals, proofs, and patterns, will be in the charge of the ENGRAVER, and at his responsibility; other officers of the Mint rendering such aid of materials and machinery as may fall within their province. These arrangements, though internal, are here openly stated, with a view to assure the public that there is a system of suitable checks and guards, against undue or secret issues. . . .

"The ensuing Rules are in plain terms, and hardly require a statement of reasons. It may be said, however, in regard to the Rule against striking a coin or pattern after its proper date, that while it seemed desirable that some patterns of former years, which are very scarce or curious should be repeated, yet we could not issue them impartially, without giving out an indefinite number. And if some kinds are thus struck, there would be a call for other kinds; there would be no knowing where to begin or end.

"Pieces struck out of date, bear a falsity on their face, and have not the interest or value of a synchronous issue. An uncertainty is also kept up, as to the extent of the supply. And in the case of regular coinage, they so far falsify the Mint Records and Tables, as to the amount of coinage and delivery, or as to the very fact of such and such pieces having been coined in any given year.

"On the whole, therefore, it seemed a plain course, to let the past go, and begin afresh. And it is a satisfaction to be able to assure all parties, that there has been no resurgent striking in the present Directorship.

"The striking of specimens in other than their proper metal, never much practiced, is to be discontinued. This irregularity has, of course, never been with unlawful intent, and never would have happened, but for the importunate desire to possess something odd, or to avoid the outlay of gold or silver. Such pieces have been struck, as patterns, from the dime of 1792 down to our day; but the united voice is now against using dies meant for gold or silver upon copper or other base metal.

"It is proper to say, that before these Rules were matured, advice was sought of several Numismatic Societies, and gentlemen skilled in this branch of study. There has not been an entire unanimity of opinion as to details, but the general tendency was toward the result as herein indicated; and it is hoped that a general approbation will be accorded . . ."

RULES

"1. No coins, nor pattern pieces, shall be struck after the year of their date; and to insure this, the dies shall be rendered unfit for that use.

"2. No coins, nor patterns, are to be issued in any but their proper metal.

"3. Any experimental or pattern piece can be obtained at the Mint, within the year of its date, but not after. Standing orders for such pieces will be registered, and attended to. Any patterns that remain on hand, at the end of the year, must be defaced: It is not desirable to make them as common as the proofs of regular coinage. If any sets of regular proofs remain over, they may be sold in the next year, but not later.

"4. The price of a pattern coin, in any but precious metal, will be three dollars in currency; if in gold or silver, the value of the metal is to be added. But when a pattern piece is adopted and used in the regular coinage, in the same year, it will then be issued as a proof, at a price near its current value; or if it comes out early in the year, it will be placed in the regular proof set. The Director reserves the right to send a pattern piece, without charge, to any incorporated Numismatic Society in the United States. In such cases, if the pattern is in gold or silver, the value of the metal will be expected.

"5. The price of the regular proof set of gold, will be forty-three dollars in gold; the proof set of silver and copper, three dollars in silver as theretofore. To suit the convenience of many, payment may be made in the currency equivalent.

"6. The profits of this whole department are reserved to the Medal Fund which is a part of the public moneys; and are not to be prerequisite to any person holding a place in the MINT. All such persons are expected to refrain from dealings in this line, or affording aid to friends or dealers outside. If this expectation is counteracted, it will call for serious notice."

Don Taxay, in his book *Counterfeit, Mis-Struck and Unofficial U.S. Coins*, (Arco), points out that the Mint workers continued to cheat even under the new rules. Proof sets were sent out which occasionally had an Uncirculated regular issue coin in the place of one of the Proofs.

Chapter 13

Augustus Saint-Gaudens' model for Liberty on the Eagle and Double Eagle was one of his favorite women. Her name was Alice Butler and he had discovered her in Windsor, Vermont, where she lived with her parents. She has been described as "tall, dark, had a classic nose, and a short, curving upper lip such as Gus (Saint-Gaudens) had never seen except on a Greek coin."

The girl was unnerved when approached by the artist, especially since there had been rumors that he had his models pose in the nude. She made it clear that only if she would always be clad would she agree to pose. She was first model for his figure Victory. She also was the model for some Greek figures he produced for the Boston Public Library, among numerous others. Although he preferred working with her over others, he apparently never had an affair with her as he did with at least one of his other models.

Index